THE SECRET OF PROGRESS

T0370699

THE SECRET OF PROGRESS

BY

W. CUNNINGHAM, F.B.A., F.S A.

FELLOW OF TRINITY COLLEGE, CAMBRIDGE
AND ARCHDEACON OF ELY
FORMERLY LECTURER IN HARVARD UNIVERSITY

CAMBRIDGE

AT THE UNIVERSITY PRESS

1918

CAMBRIDGE
UNIVERSITY PRESS

University Printing House, Cambridge CB2 8BS, United Kingdom

Cambridge University Press is part of the University of Cambridge.

It furthers the University's mission by disseminating knowledge in the pursuit of education, learning and research at the highest international levels of excellence.

www.cambridge.org
Information on this title: www.cambridge.org/9781107429024

© Cambridge University Press 1918

First published 1918
First paperback edition 2014

A catalogue record for this publication is available from the British Library

ISBN 978-1-107-42902-4 Paperback

IN AFFECTIONATE REMEMBRANCE
OF
WILLIAM JAMES

PREFATORY NOTE

I WAS much interested in Professor James's Gifford Lectures on the *Varieties of Religious Experience*; and I have ventured to try to carry on his work by sketching the development of the Spiritual Consciousness in Man. These pages have no pretensions to that thoroughness and mastery of detail which could only come from life-long concentration on such a subject; but I hope that a variety of interests and familiarity with different points of view need not be disqualifications in a writer who only aims at popular exposition.

W. C.

Trinity College, Cambridge
  8 *November* 1918

CONTENTS

I. SPIRITUAL ELEMENTS IN SUCCESS

II. THE AWAKENING OF SPIRITUAL CONSCIOUSNESS

III. THE THEOCRACY

IV. THE PSALMS

V. INTIMACY WITH GOD

VI. KINDRED SPIRITS AND COMMUNION WITH GOD

VII. THE NEW THEOCRACY

VIII. THE PERSON OF CHRIST

IX. CHRISTENDOM

I. *The Foundation*

II. *The Superstructure in the West*

III. *The Disruption of Christendom*

X. UNITED WITNESS TO CHRIST

I. *Different Denominations*

II. *Causes of Difference*

III. *Collective Effort*

THE SECRET OF PROGRESS

I

SPIRITUAL ELEMENTS IN SUCCESS

I The war has at least served to illustrate the fact that in historical times there has been an extraordinary material progress in the world. Never before in human history were such enormous resources brought into play. The masses of men, that have been organised in armies and equipped and maintained, are quite without precedent. They have also had command of weapons which possess an accuracy that was quite unknown in old days, and they have the means of dealing far-reaching destruction. When to the employment of these powers upon the land we add that we are also able to carry on war under the surface of the sea and in the air above, we begin to feel what an enormous command man now has over the resources of nature. There has been an extraordinary advance in knowledge, and this has resulted in a wonderful development of human power.

But while we see proof of the progress in resources that has occurred, we are also forced to recognise that in many ways civilisation has been a disappointment and a failure. Sixty years ago

Buckle[1] regarded it as clear that militarism and high intellectual development were not compatible: till recently, many people were prepared to believe that warfare was alien to the interest of civilised peoples and could only occur among half civilised or backward races. But this war has shown that these hopes were vain, and that the last result of civilisation was not to render war impossible, but to give the means of carrying it out on a vastly extended scale. The increase of knowledge and of power over nature, and the sense of the benefits of intercourse and inter-communication have not sufficed to give us any immunity from war.

2   The reason seems to lie in the fact that while we have advanced so much in knowledge of the means by which to give effect to our wills, there is extraordinary diversity among the wills themselves, and readiness to pursue different and incompatible objects. We could only hope for peace, if there were some common object which all nations were alike satisfied to join in pursuing; but the particular aims which call forth and direct the activities of different peoples are incompatible one with another. The aim of the Germans to be dominant and to pursue their own destiny, while other peoples minister to their material needs, does indeed open up a prospect of an unbroken peace, but of one that could only be maintained on the assumption that other peoples should relinquish

[1] *History of Civilisation,* I, 178.

the effort to pursue for themselves the ideals of life they cherish.

Self-assertion, either national or personal, is the root of the mischief which besets our civilisation, not only in war but in peace. Just as there are many peoples in the world which claim an opportunity for self-determination, so there are many individuals in every civilised community who claim a right to enjoy opportunities of self-development and regard this right as supreme, and as something which should never be subordinated to other ends. The claim to pursue particularist aims lies at the root of many of the movements of our day; while on the one hand we see an immense increase of organisation for common purposes, we find also an indisposition to accept the control that is needed in order that human activities may attain their highest efficiency. The demand of the individual for independence is inconsistent with the maintenance and working of human society; yet individual independence is idealised as if it were an absolute good by anarchists. If this claim be admitted, there seems to be little ground for expecting successful social reconstruction after the war.

3   If the war has brought out the reality of progress and the reason of the insecurity which attends it, we have also been helped to see in what direction we may look for a possible solution of the difficulties. Individual freedom and efficient organisation are both preserved in self-discipline.

The acceptance of discipline is the free determination to submit to another will, in the hope of accomplishing an ulterior purpose; and the present war has shown the possibility of discipline on an unprecedented scale. Supernatural hopes in the past inspired Mohammedan conquerors to reckless deeds of courage, and the personality of a great leader like Napoleon found a response in the devotion of his soldiers. There has been in the allied armies a wonderful recognition of a cause as well worth fighting for, and a willingness to risk everything on its behalf, which has shown itself in the morale of the armies. It is this power to transmute the human will itself, and to direct it so that it sacrifices its immediate aim, and subordinates itself to some larger ambition, and accepts an impersonal object with all its energies and activities, that has been at work in the awakening of Britain and America to their part in the struggle, and in the organisation and disciplining of their armies. In this we have seen a manifestation of the operation of spiritual power. The war has indeed shown us the extraordinary command which human beings possess over material things, but it has also brought out the importance of the human will and of the spiritual influences which mould the will. In the East a horde of men, who were drilled in the use of arms and compelled to fight has melted away, while in the West an army of disciplined men, inspired by a common enthusiasm, continued to hold their own against vast numbers. We all feel that the morale of an army is essential to its success; and we see how the Germans have recognised the importance of psychology and of the inner life, both in their deliberate efforts to stir up passion among their own people, and in a parade of physical force and its frightfulness which might break the spirit of the Allies and of Neutrals who sympathised with them.

4   The specific character of spiritual power is also commonly recognised in discussions about the coming peace and the question of its permanence. Some Germans, whose ambitions are fixed, are eager to prepare for the next war, while those who desire to live and to let live are considering under what conditions peace can be rendered permanent. Only if there is a change in national wills, and the nations pursue a common purpose, can there be a real security against animosity arising. Much ingenuity is being expended on organising a League of Nations, which shall be able to bring physical force to bear on any offender, and to compel the maintenance of peace. But any such system ultimately depends on the power of bringing physical force to bear; there is a constant change in the relative position and circumstances of different nations which renders it difficult to rely on the power of exercising external pressure. But moral influence is not dependent on circumstances; the honourable man "sweareth unto his neighbour "and disappointeth him not though it were to his

"own hindrance"; and a necessary condition of a peace that shall be permanent lies in a change of national wills, so that each nation shall not merely aim at its own aggrandizement but shall be willing to submit to some sacrifice for the sake of the good of other peoples. However publicly a promise is made, a nation may find some excuse in changed circumstances for disregarding it. We cannot be satisfied that any organisation will serve to curb the results of international animosity, or that permanent peace can be brought about so long as jealousy is nurtured. The war has shown us, even in this materialistic age, that we cannot rely on equipment or command over physical forces for attaining human welfare, but that spiritual power is essential both for victory in war and for the permanence of peace. After all a desire for improvement is the very salt of life; it initiates successful action and prevents the decay which serves to weaken so many human institutions.

5   The spiritual element in human life is well worth studying in its genesis and growth. It has attained its present influence gradually, and it is by tracing the stages in its development that we may have the best hope of understanding the conditions which make for its diffusion and growth. And it needs careful study, for though it is such an important factor, its traces do not lie on the surface and we may easily miss them altogether.

There are indeed two different standpoints from

which we may regard human life, and two distinct
habits of mind which we may form in the plans we
make for ourselves and for others. We may look
at the phenomena of human life as mere spectators,
from the outside as it were, taking account of the
records of the past or of the occurrences of the
present day, as they are presented to us. Or on the
other hand we may view human life in the light of
our own actual experience as living ourselves. The
attitude of the onlooker is that which we habitually
adopt in learning about things and thus obtaining
increased power over natural resources, and there
is a temptation to be consistent and apply it to
human life as well. But we pay for this consistency;
our knowledge of life as mere onlookers is meagre
and superficial. We cannot detect an efficient
cause at work in the world outside as clearly as we
feel the direct relation between what we determine
and what we do. It is in actual life that we feel the
influence of an inspiring ideal and can detect the
initiation of a change. There may be convenience
in treating human life in terms of *thought* and
formulating the regular sequences which may be
observed, but we can examine it more fully and
deeply when we recognise that human life can be
most appropriately described and discussed in
terms of *will*. Life as we know it is a struggle; it
only assumes a mechanical regularity when we
choose for our own convenience to break it up into
sections. There is, besides, a large field of human

experience of which, if we look at life as spectators from the outside, we can only take account very imperfectly. We may see the results of human devotion and passion, but we only hear their echoes as we read of past events or distant occurrences. They are but dim reflections of what was once a vivid experience.

The difference between these two points of view comes out most markedly when we are discussing questions of conduct. We may habituate ourselves to look at human lives as we do at the material things we use, and as cogs in the wheels of some great mechanism; but it is foolish, for the sake of consistency, to think of ourselves in this fashion. We know that we are capable of forming a purpose and of framing some ideal of life which we will endeavour to realise. In the actual present we have links both with the past and the future,—an indebtedness to bygone ages for the means of giving effect to our purpose, to our forecasts and hopes for the future for framing our ideals,—and the more we are conscious in our decisions of these influences, the more shall we be redeemed from the narrowness of a self-centred life and the better shall we be able to follow our own purpose strenuously, instead of being content to drift through life along the lines of least resistance as mere creatures of circumstances.

6   We should doubtless correct many of our errors if we were able to see ourselves as others

see us; but there would be a still greater gain if we were able to know others as intimately as we know ourselves, and to have real acquaintance with their inner lives and the feelings and aims which actuate their conduct. We can best understand the past as it actually occurred if we read it in the light of our own experience. It was not always dead, to be looked at from a distance and analysed; it consisted of the actual struggles of actual men, who were moved by passion, who cherished ideals, who sought to achieve their aims, and who succeeded or failed. It is on this account that literature has such practical value in supplementing our knowledge of history[1]; the writer gives us some insight, sometimes unconsciously, into the motives which were really at work, and which are so alien to our own habits of thought that we could not easily guess at them.

We shall have very different conceptions of the spiritual, according as we think of human life as mere onlookers or are prepared to discuss it as we know it ourselves. If as mere onlookers we take some particular experience of the sequence of cause and effect in phenomena outside us, and regard it as typical of what is universal in the orderly world around, and go back by successive steps to a Great First Cause, we find a mere abstrac-

---

[1] On the importance of taking ideas into account in attempting to explain events see Cunningham, *Growth of English Industry*, I, 17.

tion that is infinitely removed from us and from our experience of life. But if we start from our own intimate experiences of life as a struggle, the wider the area of which we take account and the larger the scale on which we examine the influences that have been brought to bear, the more shall we feel the variety and complexity of the elements which are controlled by Him in Whom we live and move and have our being.

It is when we think of ourselves as parts of the Universe, and look at the great world through our own experience, that we find common elements which connect it together[1]. The spiritual is not a mere abstraction, but a living influence, of which the working has been felt by human beings personally, and it has taken a wider and deeper hold upon mankind as the ages have passed.

7   We must at the outset recognise that any attempt to trace the development of the spiritual consciousness is a matter of extreme difficulty. Not only is there obscurity as to the data on which we can rely, but the mere statement of the problem seems to involve a paradox, if not a contradiction in terms. How can the Spiritual and Eternal have a history in time? How can the Spiritual and Universal be located in things of sense, or institutions? There can of course be no development or change in the nature of God, but

[1] G. T. Fechner, *Die Tagesansicht gegenüber der Nachtansicht,* p. 16.

there may be change in the consciousness of man.
There are differences among the individuals we
know in their power of insight, their capacity for
feeling, and their energy in devising and carrying
out lines of conduct; there have been differences in
these respects between different generations; and
the power of insight, the capacity of feeling and
energy in action have changed as the ages passed.
We are sometimes inclined to doubt whether any
real progress has been made and whether any
change in human nature has occurred throughout
the past. The powers of sense perception of the
primitive man, of sight and of all that is involved
in woodcraft, put the civilised man to shame; the
intensity of feeling, and the power of controlling
feeling exhibited by Red Indians, are not obviously
surpassed by those who are nurtured under other
conditions; but the results of his activities show
that there has at least been an extraordinary change
in the variety of man's interests, and in his capacity
for organised action. There has been growth in
man's inner life, as well as increase in his knowledge
of the world around him.

Primitive man is "immersed in nature[1]," and
restricted on all sides by physical surroundings: his
feeling that he is himself a part of physical nature is
so strong as to affect all his ways of thinking and
the terms he uses. But the civilised man is much
more responsive to the influences of ideal objects,

[1] Hegel, *Philosophy of History*, 59.

and has attained the power of creating ideals for himself. This change may have been most obvious in individuals here and there, but it has affected the average man in certain areas, and it has come about by gradual changes. It is analogous to what we ourselves know of life; and we accept this analogy when we regard human consciousness as assimilating the spiritual environment and forming new spiritual relationships, just as animal life assimilates elements from the physical surroundings and enters into new relationships with the physical world by adapting its surroundings to itself, and itself to its surroundings. The changes of man's inner life show an increasing detachment from things of sense and an increased susceptibility to the influence of the Spiritual; the belief in the possibility of intercourse with the Spiritual can be traced through all the ages, and the conscious desire for increased intercourse with the Spiritual has been constantly at work.

Though man has shown himself more susceptible to the Spiritual, it would be absurd to pretend that he has come to be merely spiritual himself, or that in the conditions of mundane life, he can ever cease to be an animal, with physical limitations to his life and powers. Indeed the world of sense is not in fundamental contradiction to the spiritual life, since it can be used to serve it: the world of sense affords the means of testing the Spiritual as true for us; we regard the Spiritual

as something we may trust, because it works in our
experience, but we are apt to fall into error when
we assume that our experience is final and complete, and deny what lies outside it. The possibility
of verification, the fact that some belief will work
has been the accepted test of truth in the knowledge
we possess of our surroundings, and this is, as
Robertson Smith pointed out, the ultimate test
that we can apply of spiritual truth. "God's
"Revelation of Himself is unfolded gradually in
"constant contact with the needs of religious life.
"Every word of God is spoken for all time, but
"every word none the less was first spoken to
"a present necessity of God's people," and was
believed because it was found to work[1].

Things of sense not only offer the sphere in which
spiritual truth is tested and confirmed, they are
the means by which truth is perpetuated. The life
of any person, the most saintly, is comparatively
short, and his influence may be very far reaching
and wide, yet it can hardly affect the world as a
whole, with the limited possibilities of communication; it is by institutions and by books, by things
in sensible forms and subject to physical conditions
that spiritual truth is perpetuated through successive generations and communicated to distant
places. Spiritual truth has been embodied in
different forms, and the development of spiritual
consciousness is the story of the manner in which

[1] W. Robertson Smith, *Old Testament* (2nd ed.), 99.

spiritual truth has been expressed in new forms, and of the success of the new forms in inspiring energy till they superseded the old. The old forms have been outgrown, because the new ones have proved more inspiring.

The literature of ancient Israel has a special interest because the writers consciously put on record the deepest aspirations of their lives, and thus enable us to see the progress of the spiritual in their world: our knowledge of external history gives us the landmarks by which we can trace the progress, in depth and range and effectiveness, of spiritual power. The more we can take our actual experience of life with us, the better shall we interpret the play of similar influences in the past. In order that we may see, we must bring a power of seeing with us; those who are blind to the influence of spiritual power in the present, cannot hope to recognise it in the occurrences of the past.

II

THE AWAKENING OF SPIRITUAL CONSCIOUSNESS

8 The continuous story of the growth of the religious consciousness of Israel begins with the call of Abraham; the earlier portions of Genesis are a prologue which deal with the world at large; while Israel in all subsequent ages looked back to Abraham as the founder of their race with whom they were in conscious connection, since they not only came from his stock but were worshippers of his God. The distinction is important since it gives a spiritual character to Israel. The supernatural character of the gods of heathen tribes who reverenced the founder of their race as himself their God, could be easily explained away[1]; but the God of Israel was not thought of as the spirit of Abraham, but as that to whom Abraham had himself looked for guidance in the present, and on whose promise for the future he had relied. The religious consciousness of the Jewish race can be traced back to his personality; but the earlier chapters of Genesis[2] are the result of reflection on the great problems of an order

[1] On Euhemerus and his philosophy of religion see Döllinger, *The Gentile and the Jew*, I, 345.

[2] The narratives are similar to those in Babylonian documents but the difference in religious character is remarkable. L. W. King, *Legends of Babylon and Egypt*, 130.

in nature, of the possibilities of self-will and passion, and of the divine destruction of evil. In the very form which they take we feel that there is repetition and other signs of a double narrative of the Creation[1], the Fall[2] and the Flood; scholarship can distinguish the manner in which this double element has been combined, but from the call of Abraham onwards, though there are occasional insertions, the narrative is more continuous. In the Bible we can trace the development of the spiritual consciousness itself, and not only find a collection of the utterances of this consciousness when it has been awakened.

This awakening is a recognition of a distinction between the world about us and a Power behind,— something that is not ourselves and that may be trusted. Clough gave expression to this faith, as it appeals to a man who is distraught by consciousness of the uncertainties and inconsistencies of the play of feeling and desire:

> It fortifies my soul to know
> That though I perish, truth is so,
> That howsoe'er I stray or range
> Whate'er I do, Thou dost not change,
> I steadier step when I recall
> That though I slip Thou dost not fall.

But primitive man was oppressed by a sense of uncertainty, not only in the world within, but in the world without. Nature, "red in tooth and

---

[1] W. Robertson Smith, *op. cit.* 415.
[2] *Ibid.* 329.

"claw," seemed to have the mastery, and there were ever present possibilities of flood or drought, of pestilence and famine, as well as of attacks from rivals in the tribal struggle for existence. There was a wonderful rest in turning from all the uncertainties of life to One Who could give guidance in the present, and on Whom it was possible to rely for the future.

In what manner this guidance was first vouchsafed we are not told, nor what served as an oracle; we only know of it as a strong conviction that led Abram to wander forth from Ur of the Chaldees; but we do know that by acting upon it, the belief in the trustworthiness of this guidance was confirmed. We are told too of the great anxiety of Abraham's life, since he had no son and his stock would become extinct; the birth of that son in his old age, and the divine acceptance of his readiness to sacrifice his dearest hopes, by the restoration of that son, confirmed his belief in the fulfilment of the promise which had been made to him. His marvellous experience could find no suitable means of recalling or recounting itself, though there was the passing away of a horror of great darkness (Genesis xv. 12). The incidents are recorded in terms of animism, there were no other terms in which such experience could be recorded at first, and we read of the intercourse of God and man, as if it were the conversation between an unfamiliar visitant and a great sheikh; but the inner convic-

tion, which remained and was handed on, was that
of the reliability of God as a guide and a keeper of
His promise, and the whole subsequent history of
Israel is the manifestation of what was involved in
this belief, though not yet expressed or understood.

9   The belief in the reliability of God's promise
was confirmed in the minds of Isaac and Jacob
by their own experience of guidance, in the successful journey of Isaac to his father's people, and in the
deliverance of Jacob from his brother's jealousy;
and we see that they attained to a fuller conception
of God, not only as *reliable*, but as *bounteous* and
accessible. Jacob's dream represented Him as a
present help. The expectation of what God could
do for His people here and now comes out more and
more fully in the blessings which Isaac pronounced
on his deathbed, and in the benedictions of Jacob[1].
And Joseph, in looking back on the wonderful
change in his own lot and on the manner in which
he had been raised up to be the means of saving
his father and brethren from destruction by famine[2],
felt that his father's God, in the fulfilment of His
promise, was able not only to bestow blessings but
to bring good out of evil. "As for you," he said to
his brethren, "ye thought evil against me : but God

---

[1] Driver assigns the tribal blessings in Genesis xlix, with
their topographical allusions, to the time of the Judges.
Genesis, 380.

[2] Jeremiah disparages the revelations given by dreams
as compared with prophecy (Jer. xxiii. 25–28).

"meant it unto good, to bring to pass, as it is this
"day, to save much people alive" (Gen. l. 20). The
purpose attributed to God is still the fulfilment of
the promise, and the raising up of a great tribe,
and there is a more definite recognition of the
bounty which He can bestow, and of new means of
obtaining guidance from Him.

I O   Moses appears to have had a still deeper
sense of God's presence as an abiding help,
in the uncertainties of his own life in exile; and at
the Burning Bush he felt himself commissioned to
return to his own people and strive to waken them
to the same faith and hope in their distresses.
"Thus shalt thou say unto the children of Israel,
"The Lord God of your fathers, the God of Abra-
"ham, the God of Isaac, and the God of Jacob, hath
"sent me unto you"..."Go, and gather the elders
"of Israel together, and say unto them, The Lord
"God of your fathers"..."appeared unto me, saying,
"I have surely visited you, and seen that which is
"done to you in Egypt: and I have said, I will
"bring you up out of the affliction of Egypt unto
"the land of the Canaanites,"..."unto a land
"flowing with milk and honey. And they shall
"hearken to thy voice" (Ex. iii. 15–18). We read
of the reluctance of Moses to undertake the task,
and how he was at length re-assured so as to attempt
it. The immediate task that lay before him was
that of facing Pharaoh himself, but there would be
still more difficulty in awakening the people to a

confidence in God as ready to fulfil the ancient promise, and in persuading them to cut themselves adrift from Egypt and to follow him as their leader into the Wilderness on a great migration to the land of promise.

During their sojourn in Egypt the descendants of Jacob had greatly increased in numbers, and the tradition of divine help and guidance that had been given to their forefathers had grown dim; but through the instrumentality of Moses it became a faith and hope in which the whole people shared, and on which they acted, with Pharaoh's terrified acquiescence, "Rise up, and get you forth from "among my people, both ye and the children of "Israel; and go, serve the Lord, as ye have said. "Also take your flocks and your herds, as ye have "said, and be gone" (Ex. xii. 31, 32). There had been a sense of oppression and wrong which was common to the whole people; and now there was a sense of a supernatural deliverance, which was sealed to them in their escape from Egypt, and prepared them for facing the perils of wandering in the wilderness and of conquering the land to which they looked as their goal.

The experience of deliverance and guidance, and of the reliability of God in fulfilling His promise had now become the common experience of the Israelites, instead of being the personal experience of one or other of the patriarchs; and the Paschal feast was instituted that this deliverance should never be forgotten, but that the memory of God's exercise of power on their behalf should be maintained for all generations.

The Israelites learned to look back on the years of wandering as a time when they were as a tribe directly dependent on God for sustenance and for guidance; S. Paul recalled the manna as God-given food, the water that came from the rock, and the pillar of cloud which gave them guidance (1 Cor. x. 1–4). The phraseology of Exodus and Deuteronomy brings out the way in which the people themselves seem to have regarded their experiences; they seem to have thought of God as participating in all the incidents of their lives. He had delivered them from Egypt, and when they fought against Amalek, He was fighting on their side. He had guided them so that they escaped the necessity of facing an encounter till they were prepared to meet it (Ex. xiii. 17); and the actual confidence of some of them in His present help is brought out in the story of Caleb, while we see that murmuring against His guidance and turning back in their hearts into Egypt was the prevailing habit of those who had no confidence in Him, despite the experiences they had enjoyed.

When faith and reliance on God thus became tribal, and were the expression of the common experience of a people, religion assumed a new character; it became externalised, so as to appeal to many individuals, and to be maintained in many generations. The renewal of the covenant with the people of Israel at Sinai was signalised by the promulgation of commands for all, through the voice of Moses; the ark was the dwelling of God among His people, the tabernacle was the tent of meeting, and the priests were those who approached Him on behalf of the people, and who gave decisions between the people when any occasion of dispute arose. The work of Moses was a double work; he not only awoke in the people the faith in God as dwelling among them, but he also gave an external form to their response to God, and rendered it possible for religion to grow and be perpetuated in the world. The evidence of the spiritual power which was exercised through him lies in that which the people were able to do; they did emerge from the condition of down-trodden slaves in Egypt; they did brace themselves to pass through the great and terrible wilderness, and to attack the Canaanites who were settled in a fertile country. There was under Moses an awakening of the spiritual consciousness of the whole nation: from this time onwards we can distinguish its external side from the inner life, and trace the changes in organisation as well as in belief and in the sense of homage and duty.

III

THE THEOCRACY

11   The life of the children of Israel went through two great changes after their wanderings ceased. The settlement in the promised land involved an alteration in their habits of life, and this was the beginning of a long series of changes in organisation and administration, in which there was a trend towards greater centralisation.

The economic changes which were consequent on the conquest must have been much more striking in some districts than in others. There were districts which were specially suited for sheep farming, and where the settlers retained, as a pastoral tribe, much of the ways of life to which they had been habituated as nomads; the tribes of Gad and Reuben and half the tribe of Manasseh continued their old avocations, and the district round Bethlehem continued to be a centre for shepherd life, in the days of David and till the time of our Lord. In other districts the tribes could enter at once into the facilities which had been prepared for them by the people they had conquered, and pursue more intensive cultivation, of cereal crops and of the vine; there were vineyards near Shiloh and dances at the vintage feast (Jud. xxi. 21). Here is at least an analogy to the conquest of Roman Britain by the

English tribes, and to the manner in which our
forefathers adopted and perpetuated methods of
cultivation, and the practice of fruit-growing which
seems to have been introduced in Roman times.
Just as our forefathers dispensed with trade and
used the Roman roads as boundaries rather than
means of communication, so do we find in Israel
little traces of commerce and of the changes in
society which it tends to produce, till it was fostered
by the kings. There are hints, here and there, which
help us to trace gradual changes in the structure of
society which correspond to those which have
occurred in our own land; there are signs of settlement in communities and pastoral districts which
gave the best opportunity for this social form to
survive with the occasions it afforded for large
gatherings (2 Sam. xiii. 23), while we read in later
times of large arable farms (2 Kings iv. 8, 18), and
of agreements between the proprietors and culti-
vators (S. Luke xvi. 7). The division of employ-
ments and industrial organisation, was doubtless
stimulated as time went on by the development of
trade. The allusions to the familiar conditions of
life in our Lord's day which we find in the parables,
make us feel how greatly society had changed its
economic character before His day since the time
of the settlement under Joshua.

12   The tendency towards centralisation had
gone some way, both in military, judicial
and religious organisation, and at length the con-

quest of Jerusalem enabled David to use that city as a centre for administration of every kind. There had been a concentration of functions in the person of the king, before Jerusalem became the local centre both for judicial purposes and for worship; but it was in the kingdom of David and Solomon that the theocracy attained its greatest prosperity, and that the sense of the presence of God with His people became stronger than it had ever been before.

Tribal organisation had ceased to suffice for military necessities; there was no longer occasion to force a passage through the country of another people, but there was need for the Israelites to defend their own country against foreign raids or attempts to reduce it to permanent subjection, and the song of Deborah shows how inefficient tribal organisation proved even in a great emergency. It was not easy to get the tribes to act together in a common cause. "Gilead abode beyond Jordan: and "why did Dan remain in ships? Asher continued "on the sea shore" (Judges v. 17). Once and again there was a combination of invaders who threatened to bring the whole nation into subjection, and to deprive them of the sense of divine protection which was bound up with their consciousness of national independence. The danger of being subjected to or absorbed by heathen powers, was a danger of ceasing to be a witness to divine power, and of losing their own sense of the sufficiency of divine protection. It was, as Deborah felt, His

cause that was at stake, and reluctance to join in
His victory was a mark of profound indifference to
Him which she deplored. "Curse ye Meroz,...curse
"ye bitterly the inhabitants thereof; because they
"came not to the help of the Lord, to the help of
"the Lord against the mighty." The defects of the
tribal system were obvious; it was at all events
subordinate in Saul's battles against the Philis-
tines (1 Sam. xiii. 2); and David's reorganisation
of the military system (2 Sam. xviii. 1, xxiii. 8)
provided much more effective central control.

The need of an improvement in the exercise of
judicial functions is equally apparent. The Levites
appear to have been recognised as the depositaries
of national custom and claimed to exercise this
function, though prophets appeared from time to
time who exercised a supreme control and "judged
Israel"; but the reign of Saul tells of a conflict of
authority, and of a rivalry between the newly
appointed king and the prophet Samuel. It was
part of the great success of David, that he not only
completed the conquest and protected the area of
the promised land by controlling neighbouring
peoples, but that his friendly relations with the
priests of Nob enabled him to do so much to set
internal distractions at rest; but the difficulties of
the administration of justice continued, and the
grievances in this matter were taken advantage of
by Absalom in fomenting rebellion. "Oh," he said,
"that I were made judge in the land, that every

"man which hath any suit or cause might come
"unto me, and I would do him justice" (2 Sam. xv.
4). It is in this connection that we may feel the
political importance of the judgment of Solomon,
"All Israel heard of the judgment which the king
"had judged; and they feared the king: for they
"saw that the wisdom of God was in him to do
"judgment" (1 Kings iii. 28).

It was thus that the Theocracy attained its
highest development, and the presence of God
among His people was recognised as giving prosperity
to the realm, and authority to the kings as the
instruments through which He gave effect to His
Will. David fought in the battles but he felt that
God had given him the victory and had won them;
and Solomon was enabled to rise to the difficulties
of ruling the great kingdom which he felt so keenly
(1 Kings iii. 7, 8). "God gave Solomon wisdom and
"understanding exceeding much, and largeness of
"heart" (1 Kings iv. 29).

The conception of a Divine Theocracy, in the
government of which God had a direct part, is one
with which we are not in complete sympathy; we
can appreciate the connection of the destiny of
Israel and the triumph of God's cause in the world,
but the language which speaks of God as a conquering monarch and of His glory as the ultimate
aim is apt to seem derogatory to Him. In a similar
way we find the importance attached to different
forms of crime confusing; the murmuring of the

children of Israel, though directed against Moses, was really a sign of want of trust in God as their present guide, and the personal assumption of supernatural powers was the form of evil which Saul endeavoured to put down in his crusade against witchcraft. A slight against God as the supreme ruler, appeared discernible to Saul in Jonathan's personal expedition and disregard of the vow which his father had made (1 Sam. xiv. 27, 44); there seemed to be a danger of forfeiting the divine blessing on which he relied for victory. David had maintained his high respect for the Lord's anointed, under the greatest difficulties in the time of Saul (2 Sam. i. 14), and with the change in his fortunes he was inspired to rise to his responsibilities. The same feeling of the close connection between the king and people in their relation to God is illustrated by the story of his sin in numbering the people, and thus showing a personal pride in his royal resources and reliance on them (2 Sam. xxiv. 3), and of the subsequent punishment which fell upon the people. "I have sinned," as David confessed, "and I have done "wickedly; but these sheep, what have they done?" (2 Sam. xxiv. 17).

1 3   Centralisation was not so completely carried out in national worship as it seems to have been in military organisation and judicial administration, involving as they did a new fiscal system which was resented as oppressive on the succession

of Rehoboam (1 Kings xii. 14, 18). The removal of
the ark from Shiloh to Jerusalem was the crowning
act in David's consolidation of the realm, and
Solomon carried out the scheme for building a
national temple in the proximity of the royal
palace with unexampled magnificence, but this
great development of the worship which had been
centred at Shiloh, did not supersede the local
sanctuaries. These survived; neither Solomon nor
Hezekiah did away altogether with the high places;
Jeroboam organised the ancient sanctuary at
Bethel as a rival to Jerusalem, and the sanctuary
at Dan, the origin of which was comparatively
recent, was also reorganised (Judges xviii. 14–31).
It was only when the institution of a synagogue
system could be provided to meet local religious
needs, that the attempt to make Jerusalem not only
the place for national festivals, but the exclusive
centre for sacrifice could be attempted with success.

Still the formation of a permanent centre of
national worship was a very great step; it had an
enormous importance in fixing a definite place
which was felt to be the centre of the Theocracy,
and the dwelling-place of God Himself, as well as of
the earthly ruler. It was the purpose which David
cherished as the object of all his endeavours, and
the devout thoughts which were associated with
the Temple find expression in Solomon's prayer;
its fortunes, its desecration and its reconstruction
are the prominent features in the story of the
Theocracy and its decadence.

IV

THE PSALMS

14 In the Psalter there is a wonderful collection of materials which give us evidence as to the inner lives of men who between them occupied a long series of years; they shared in the faith of Abraham, and believed that the God whom they worshipped was bounteous to the covenanted people and present among them. Taken together the Psalms give us evidence as to the inner life of Israel; each individual Psalmist endeavoured to give expression to his own experience—to the gratitude which he felt to God for His gifts and guidance, to his own sense of failure, to his desire to seek after God, his hope to find Him, and his wish to do God's will; he tells, too, the personal message which seemed to come to him as guidance from God. Each of these expressions of devout feeling is quick and powerful; it is the effort to put on record a vivid personal experience; and as we read and ponder it, a similar feeling may be awakened in our hearts.

We can often see how the power of sympathy affects and carries away many individuals in a crowd. There is a sort of infection which influences one after another so that a common wave of feeling runs through all. Similarly our sympathy may bridge the gulf which separates us from persons who lived hundreds of years ago; by following their words, we may enter into their thoughts and aspirations so as to feel them for ourselves. The awakening of personal devout feeling, as an echo of vivid devout feeling in the distant past, is a sure way of fostering and stimulating religious activities.

The Psalms were used with this object for many generations, and in various separate collections, before they were brought together in their present form and arrangement in our Psalter. While this long period of habitual use testifies to the spiritual value which men of bygone ages found in the Psalms, it has put difficulties in the way of those who would wish to get as closely as possible at the circumstances under which each Psalm was written, and the personal experience which it expresses. Many of those who admire Cardinal Newman's hymn "Lead kindly Light" are glad that the story has been preserved as to the Mediterranean voyage during which it was written[1], and they are grateful when similar information can be given about other favourite hymns. So there would be a great satisfaction if we could understand the conditions under which each Psalm was composed, and we should appreciate them better. But the treatment which they have received during five hundred years of collection and use renders this task very difficult.

[1] J. H. Newman, *Apologia pro vita sua.* Edited by W. Ward, p. 135.

There is need of much accurate work by scholars in order to enable us to understand each of the Psalms better and appreciate it more truly; but every one of us, even though we may have no pretensions to keep up with recent theories, may try to avail himself of the results which are generally accepted by scholars.

The titles which are affixed to most of the Psalms in the first and second books are not to be trusted in their tradition of authorship, but they are excellent evidence in regard to the use which was made of the Psalter. Sometimes they are musical directions showing that the Psalm was sung, as they specify that there was an accompaniment with string instruments (Ps. iv) or with wind instruments (Ps. v). In others there seems to be the name of the melody to which the words could be sung (Pss. ix, xxii, xlv). These titles also testify to the long continued use of the Psalms. The final collection took place before the translation of the Septuagint about 130 B.C. But some of these titles seem to have been unintelligible to the translators; and therefore the Psalms, which these titles designate, must have been ancient hymns even then. If the tradition which ascribes any of them to David is correct, and we have independent evidence as to his reputation as a poet and musician (2 Sam. vi. 5, 14), the preservation and devout use of the Psalms, which were ultimately collected together, extended over a period of hundreds of years.

However reverent and careful the use of a sacred book may be, there is a certain amount of wear and tear which cannot be avoided. A Prayer Book which has come down in a family for a generation or two may have some loose pages, and the names in the Prayer for the Royal Family at least are likely to be altered so as to bring them up to date; and it is to be expected that similar incidents might occur in regard to a written roll and affect the text of subsequent copies, so as to leave traces of omissions or alterations.

The titles also show that the Psalms were formerly grouped together in ways that were convenient for their use. There were some which contained the repertoire of a particular choir like the sons of Asaph or the sons of Korah. There were others that were used on special occasions, like the Hallel (Pss. cxiii–cxviii) and the Pilgrimage Songs (Pss. cxx–cxxxiv). It does not appear that the Israelites before the time of Ezra had any pedantic sense of the need for copying a roll accurately. They seem to have had no scruple about altering an ancient Psalm to fit it for use on some new occasion or even in accordance with a change of taste, and we can hardly attribute the grouping together of Elohistic Psalms to any other motive. In just the same way there is frequent complaint nowadays of the manner in which hymns have been altered by editors who wished to make them more suitable for a special collection, and did not attach great importance to the duty of perpetuating the author's words as he wrote them.

There is also reason to believe that the Psalms were arranged and divided for the convenience of regular use, so as to form a cycle of songs which corresponded with the cycle of lections into which the Pentateuch had been divided[1]. There are combinations and repetitions of Psalms which are almost unaccountable unless we suppose that the final collection was divided into portions in this way; thus it is that the conditions of use have introduced much confusion, and there is great difficulty in recovering the original form of each Psalm or the conditions and the experience which it expresses. Scholarship has no need to plead for some special justification as a legitimate exercise of human faculties, since it can increasingly render the service of clearing away this confusion, so as to make the Psalms more available for devout use. There is no occasion for the Gelehrte[2], either German or English, to be supercilious and to treat scholarly study as something superior, which is to be pursued for its own sake; whereas it attains its highest value when it is pursued as a means to the practical use of the Bible.

[1] King, *The Psalms in Three Collections*. Introduction to the third Collection.

[2] A story is told of a well-known Cambridge professor who stammered badly; a German friend had remarked to him that there seemed to be no word for Gelehrte in English and he replied, "Oh yes we have a word; we call them p-p-prigs."

15 A very little attention serves to show that the Psalms differ very much in character. Some were obviously composed to be sung publicly on great occasions. We can feel that the xxivth Psalm is appropriate to the translation of the Ark to Jerusalem, while there are others which seem to be specially connected with the restored Temple. Besides these choral odes there are others which are personal in character, like the morning and evening prayers (Pss. iv, v) which are regarded as among the oldest Psalms in the book. Many are songs; some of them are dirges, while others have a festal character. Others are poems of a literary character, such as the Acrostic Psalms; but in all of them there is the employment of the antiphonal response which is characteristic of Hebrew poetry. It is at least worth while to be familiar with the structure of a Psalm, and this is indicated in the *Golden Treasury Psalter*, in accordance with Ewald's treatise on the Psalms, which is very accessible to English readers[1] and is epoch making, not because the results he reached were in any sense final, but because he has set such an inspiring example of the devout study, which we may each pursue for ourselves.

Ewald has also attempted to determine the manner in which the different psalms may be

[1] It is reproduced not only in the translation of Ewald's work but in the *Psalms Chronologically arranged by Four Friends*, and in the *Golden Treasury Psalter*.

distributed over the eight hundred years, which elapsed between the time of David and the final arrangement and editing of the Psalter, when the opportunity of touching up and altering psalms in accordance with current use ceased. The traditional practice had been to connect somewhat arbitrarily the various psalms with incidents in the life of David to which they seemed appropriate[1]; but such identifications are not convincing, and leave us in uncertainty even in cases where we have much more detailed information than we possess in regard to the life of David. The story of Canute, as it has been preserved in the *Liber Eliensis*[2], gives us an instance of a royal singer whose songs were his best memorial.

"The Abbot of Ely, being one of the three great "Abbots who held the office and dignity of the "King's Chancellor, each of them taking it in their "course four Months in the year; King *Canute* "several times took the occasion of our Abbot's "entering on his office, which was always on the "Purification of the Virgin *Mary*, to keep that "Feast with the usual solemnity at the Abby of "*Ely*. Once it happened, in his passage thither by "water, with *Emma* his Queen, being attended by "many of his Nobles; as they drew near to *Ely*

[1] The title to Ps. vii does not refer to any incidents recorded in the books of Samuel, but is derived from an independent tradition.

[2] J. Bentham, *History of the Cathedral Church of Ely*, p. 94.

"the King was standing up and taking a view of
"the Church, which was directly before him; and
"whilst he was musing upon it, he perceived a kind
"of harmonious sound at a great distance, which
"at first he could not tell what to make of; but
"finding it to increase as he advanced; he listened
"attentively to it, and perceived it to be the Monks
"in the Church singing their canonical hours. The
"King in the joy of his heart broke out into a Song
"which he made extempore on the occasion, calling
"on the Nobles that were about him to join in the
"chorus. This song in the *English* or *Saxon* lan-
"guage, as used at the time, was long preserved by
"the Ely Monks, for the sake of the Royal Author;
"we have only the first stanza handed down to us:

> Pleasantly sang the monks in Ely
> When Canute the King rowed by,
> 'Row Knights near the land
> 'And hear ye the song of the monks[1].'

"They continued singing till they arrived at land;
"and soon after the Monks met the King, and
"conducted him in solemn procession into the
"Church."   The lines by themselves, apart from
this record of the incident, would have left us in
doubt whether it was the king's intention to divert
the rowers from the course they were taking or to
hurry them on towards their intended destination.

A sounder method consists in the careful study

---

[1] The translation is from H. Morley's *English Writers*, I,
468.

of the allusions,—especially of the allusions which show whether the city of Jerusalem was standing, and whether there was organised worship at the Temple. By applying this test, in conjunction with his judgment on the characteristic style of different authors, Ewald has attempted to rearrange all the psalms in the chronological order in which they were written. His views on this point have not met with general acceptance though the principle on which he lays stress is very instructive, and enables us at least to get an approximate arrangement which applies to many psalms and tells us the circumstances under which they were written. The allusions to times of warfare and of triumph are very noticeable; Psalm xviii seems appropriate to the victories of David, while Psalms xlvi, xlvii and xlviii may be more naturally "referred "to the deliverance of Jerusalem from the Assyrians "under Sennacherib in 701 B.C.[1]." The language of Psalms lxxiv and lxxix seems appropriate to the persecution of Antiochus Epiphanes and Psalm cxlix to the first victories of the Maccabees[2].

We can distinguish psalms which reflect the times of the decadent monarchy and divine judgment, of the Captivity, and of the reorganisation of the worship at the Temple on lines laid down in the Law. These events mark three great crises which divide up the long ages when the Psalms were

---

[1] Kirkpatrick, *Psalms*, p. xl.
[2] W. Robertson Smith, *op. cit.* 210.

used, and enable us to place them in groups;
while affinities of literary style may enable scholars
to detect their relations with greater precision.

16   In so far as the Psalms can be approximately
        assigned to periods in the history of Israel,
we need no longer take them separately as if they
were each independent, for we can compare them
with other examples of contemporary literature,
and pay attention to their relations; we are better
able to note similarities of thought and of phraseology, and to trace the recurrence of similar
metaphors. This sort of comparison is interesting
and suggestive, for three great branches of the
literature of Israel are closely connected; the
prophets have put on record their insight into the
purpose and character of God; the psalms are the
expression of human response to the God thus
made known more fully; while the Histories,
including the Law, give us information about the
external conditions of the Theocracy and the
changes which occurred from century to century.
The Old Testament writings are closely intercon-
nected, and strengthen one another like a threefold
cord. There may be a better understanding of each
Psalm, or the message of each prophet, when we
are familiar with the external condition of the
people at the time they were composed; and the
Psalms give us a key by which we may trace the
character of the devout feeling that underlay and
gave rise to the incidents which have been recorded.

The connection of the messages of the prophets with the response of the psalmists is closely exemplified in comparing Pss. xlvi and xlviii with the utterances of the prophet Isaiah to Hezekiah, and Ps. xxxi with Jeremiah's sense of his mission and the opposition with which he had to contend. The psalms of the exiles express a sense of the burden of sin (Pss. xxii and xxxv) and remind us of Isaiah liii, and also show something of the prophet's attachment to and hopes for his own land (Pss. cii, cxxi). The correspondence between the Psalms and the literature of the Restoration, such as the books of Ezra and Nehemiah and the prophecies of Haggai and Zechariah, is very close, not only in the delight in the Temple (Ps. cxviii) and reverence for the Law (Ps. cxix), but in the confident expectation that the God of Israel would prove Himself to be the guide and ruler of all mankind (Pss. lxviii, xcvi). When the age of prophecy had passed we find affinities with the Wisdom[1] literature in Ps. xlix and its sense of the peaceful felicity of the pious[2].

Through careful study the Psalms may cease to be a mere collection of materials gathered haphazard, and may become a series of monuments for the religious history of Israel; we can find an increasing detachment from the divine institutions which had been organised in the time of David,

---

[1] On the lasting importance of this habit of mind see Döllinger, *The Gentile and the Jew*, ii, 383, 405.

[2] W. Robertson Smith, *op. cit.* 210.

and a greater prominence given to the personal religious life of the individual; there was a deeper sense of sin, and of God's care for the people who were restored to their own land. Religious hopes were no longer so closely bound up with the maintenance of the line of David, while provision is made for fostering the religious life of those who were dispersed among heathen lands and thus cut off from immediate participation in the customs which characterised the land of Israel and the city of Jerusalem.

V

INTIMACY WITH GOD

17 In his excellent work on the Old Testament in the Jewish Church, Dr Robertson Smith occasionally used language which has apparently not been quite well considered, and may at any rate give rise to misconception. He definitely repudiates the view that religion is merely based on opinions about God[1], which have become increasingly abstract as men have taken wider views of the Universe, and points out that the Bible is "a book of Experimental Religion[2]"; but he speaks as if the subjective element could be definitely distinguished from the externals of religion, and of the subjective element as unchanging and true, while the ritual and ordinances and literature of religion are human and liable to change. "These are the subjective elements of "religion, the answer of the believing heart to God. "And precisely in these elements the religion of all "ages is much alike[3]."

When we come to consider the prophets, however, we find that this way of putting the matter is misleading; we need to distinguish among the subjective elements, and we find that those which

[1] W. Robertson Smith, *op. cit.* 295.   [2] *Op. cit.* 8.
[3] *Op. cit.* 191.

are of most importance are alive and growing; they are not unchanging. We are brought face to face with a great change in the inner consciousness of the prophets, we need to try and distinguish the nature of a change that occurred in the subjective elements of religion; they felt that they themselves enjoyed an intimacy with God to which the founders of the nation had made no claim, and the reality of this intimacy was acknowledged at least by those who complained at a later time that the age of prophecy had ceased.

The prophets thought of themselves as admitted into the inner circle of God's servants[1], and as taken into His confidence in regard to His purposes for His people. The secret of the Lord is with them that fear Him. Just as the servants of an earthly ruler were taken into His confidence and might prove unworthy of the trust, so the prophets believed that they had been summoned into the immediate presence of God, and the consciousness of the privilege that had been granted them was overwhelming. They felt that they had clearer insight than other men and could speak with divine authority, and that they were commissioned by God to declare to other men the truth they had received, however unwelcome it might be. This sense of intimacy with God, gave a new character to their own faith. They felt themselves to be privileged above other men and this influenced the

[1] Cf. 2 Kings vi. 8, 9, Esther i. 13, 14.

manner in which they gave utterance to their sense of the destiny of the chosen people, and dismissed time-servers with contempt.

18 Each prophet seems to have looked back on the time when he was first admitted into the circle of God's intimate friends and given insight into His purpose, as the great turning-point in his life. Amos, in the prosperous times of the northern kingdom under Jeroboam II, had experienced something like the conversion of George Fox. "The Lord took me as I followed the flock, and "the Lord said unto me, Go, prophesy unto my "people Israel" (Amos vii. 15). In similar fashion Isaiah looked back on the year when King Uzziah died, as the time when the commission came to him to denounce the sins of Jerusalem (Is. vi. 1), and Jeremiah is equally precise as to the time when he realised that he was God's chosen instrument, incapable as he felt of fulfilling the task assigned him[1] (Jer. i. 1, 6). This divine call came to men who had not prepared themselves for such work.

Even in modern times we occasionally come across traditional lore about the interpretation of the trivialities of life, and the light they throw on the designs of some supernatural power; there are those who can interpret what is adumbrated by meeting three magpies, or the precise nature of the danger incurred by going under a ladder. This kind

[1] Sanday, *Inspiration*, 149.

of learning which consisted in the interpretation of
signs was greatly developed in all countries in
ancient times; soothsayers were constantly con-
sulted, there were wise men and sorcerers who
withstood Moses at the court of Pharaoh (Ex. vii.
11), and magicians, astrologers, sorcerers and
Chaldeans who complained that Nebuchadnezzar
was unreasonable in the demands he made upon
them (Dan. ii. 10). The science of interpreting
signs from the flight of birds, or the entrails of
sacrifices, or from flashes of lightning was highly
developed among the Etruscans[1], and continued to
be practised in connection with public affairs at
Rome under the Empire. Apparently the sons of
the prophets in Israel might undergo an apprentice-
ship to some similar profession; but Amos dis-
claimed such training altogether. "I was no
"prophet, neither was I a prophet's son" (Amos vii.
14). He did not profess any skill in the interpretation of signs, but claimed to speak for God Himself;
it was not the special and the exceptional that he
noted, but the purpose and mind of the eternal
God. He was conscious of this insight while in the
possession of his ordinary powers, not in moments
of special excitement and frenzy. The soothsayers
in Israel, who professed to interpret the signs of
Jehovah's favour or anger (1 Sam. ix. 9), were also
advisers to whom an appeal might be made in the
hope of relieving anxieties; but there was all the

[1] Döllinger, *The Gentile and the Jew*, ii. 4, 99–106.

difference in the world between those who depended on their skill to interpret signs, and those who claimed, as the prophets did, to have been taken into the confidence of God Himself.

The legitimacy of this claim was recognised in Israel from the time of Moses onwards, and there was a general recognition, after the study of the law as the normal rule of life had begun, that this gift had been withdrawn; but there might be much dispute as to whether any particular man could justify his personal pretensions to speak with divine authority (1 Kings xxii. 7). Just because the prophet gave no sign, as Moses had done, but only delivered his bare word, there was room for much dispute as to his authority; ability to foretell the future was the only test available (Deut. xviii. 22) of his insight into the divine mind, though this test might not be immediately applicable. But when his authority was admitted, extraordinary weight was attached to his message, for he declared the mind of God Himself, not a mere prediction about a future occurrence but a truth for all time.

19   The prophets had a message for their own time—a time of great commercial prosperity, and of the growth of commercial empires[1]; but they were not mere opportunists who could read the signs of the times; they had a message to give in regard to the social difficulties and the political

[1] On the condition of Jerusalem at the time when Isaiah began his prophecies see G. A. Smith, *Isaiah*, 1, 20.

questions of their own day, which comes home to
us when we try to face the similar struggles of our
own time. We may enter into the personal feeling
of Moses in his sense of weakness, or of David in the
confession of his sin, but they had no experience
of times like ours; whereas the prophets were called
on to play the part of politicians and social reformers.

This gave them a wider outlook than some of
their contemporaries, for they were conscious that
the God of Israel, was not merely the ruler of their
nation, but the God of all the earth, who would
correct the overweening ambition of the great
despots who wielded enormous power. His judgment had been exercised in the deliverance from
Sennacherib of Jerusalem, as the centre whence
His Holiness emanated[1]; and similar judgments
were pronounced against one or another of the
great oriental empires, and against the commercial
city of Tyre. These prophets had visions of the
righteousness of God triumphing over the resources which man heaped up, and the pride he
took in his achievements; faith in the power of
Right to assert itself over Might has sustained the
oppressed in all generations since they gave it
voice. They were bitterly opposed and denounced,
however, in their own day, because they refused to
believe that the chosen people were in any way
exempt from God's judgments, or could rely on

[1] W. Robertson Smith, *op. cit.* 364.

His promise to David as giving them immunity
from obedience to Him (Is. ii. 8, 9, 18, 20; xxx. 22;
xxxi. 7). Isaiah had hoped for a destruction of
idolatry and a reform of the ancient realm; but
though the reform which was effected on the lines
laid down in Deuteronomy had been real, it was
only temporary, and the hope of it passed away
with the death of Josiah. Jeremiah realised how
deep the corruption of the realm had gone, and
that there must be a divine discipline for the
chosen people, in order that they might be fitted
to carry out their divine mission in the world. He
could not anticipate any escape from the divine
judgments for those who relied on the promises to
David; Isaiah had strengthened the resistance to
an invader, but Jeremiah seemed to play the part
of a traitor, in proclaiming the imminence of a
divine discipline for the city of David and in protesting that the truth of God's promise was not an
assurance of the inviolability of Jerusalem for all
time and under all circumstances. An earlier age
had taken for granted that the acknowledgment of
Jehovah was a protection from disaster and that
prosperity must be the guerdon of those whom
God had chosen as His people, but the prophets
had insight to see that the servant of Jehovah
might be called to suffer, that destruction was
coming upon the people, and that only a remnant
would survive to carry on the witness for God in
the world. Jeremiah was able to expose the vanity

of the hopes of those who believed in God as one
who would grant His chosen people opportunity
to continue in sin, instead of leading them to re-
nounce their sin, and to set forth His Righteousness.

Under the influence of this wider apprehension of
the rule of God over all the Earth, and the deeper
apprehension of His purpose for His own people,
the prophets outlived the traditional trust in the
line of David as a pledge of divine protection, and
cherished a faith in God as one who could accom-
plish His purpose despite apparent failure.

20   Their sense of intimacy with God not only
gave the prophets a claim to speak with
authority on burning political questions and the
need of national discipline, it kept alive a constant
feeling of what was required of themselves personally. They taught that the nation must strive to
live up to its special privileges, and that the special
privileges which had come to them as prophets of
God gave them no claim to special indulgence. The
very idea of converse with the Holy God, involved
consecration and purity[1], and though it might
involve the loneliness of those who sought to cut
themselves off from evil surroundings, it had a
great reward. "Thy word," said Jeremiah, "was
"unto me the joy and rejoicing of my heart; for I
"am called by thy name, O Lord God of hosts"
(Jer. xv. 16); and the prophet had a sense of power
which sustained him in his task. "But truly," said

---

[1] W. Robertson Smith, *op. cit.* 289.

Micah, "I am full of power by the spirit of the "Lord, and of judgment, and of might, to declare "unto Jacob his transgression, and unto Israel his "sin" (Micah iii. 8). The truth which they proclaimed was something to live by, even when they abandoned the certainty of local protection from God and realised that Zion must be plowed like a field and Jerusalem become heaps.

The more we study the claims and character of the prophets the better shall we understand the controversies which arose among the Jews about S. John the Baptist; we shall feel, too, how completely our Lord fulfilled the character of a prophet both in His mission, and in His conscious relation to God, as well as in His joy in the sense that He had finished the work that was given Him to do.

VI

KINDRED SPIRITS AND COMMUNION WITH GOD

2 1 Since the time in the wilderness when Moses welcomed the prophesying of Eldad and Medad in the Camp there had been a tradition that any of the Lord's people might be called upon to exercise the prophetic office; and many of those who claimed no special commission from Him were yet conscious of an inner life where they had communion with God. The destruction of Jerusalem, and the withdrawal of the special mission of the prophets, alike contributed to a diffusion of this sense of the devout life as a privilege which all Israelites might enjoy, and of which exile could not deprive them.

The Temple services had been abandoned when the people were carried into captivity, and in a heathen land there was no temptation for the pious Israelite to resort to local sanctuaries. In their own land the local worship had long continued and it was only in the time of Josiah that a serious attempt was made to treat high places as unsanctioned for worship and to put them down. But the pious Israelites during the exile, and throughout their dispersion were deprived of the opportunity

of engaging in Sacrifice, and habits were formed of
regular worship, of praise and petition, in which
nothing could be offered but the devotion of the
heart. And Daniel is an example of those who
found supreme satisfaction in such devotional
practices, with the thought of Jerusalem kept before
him and the hours of the morning and evening
sacrifice kept in mind, but with no regard to the
physical conditions which had been considered to
be essential to access to the presence of God.

The exiles were cut off too from the surroundings
and habits of religious men; they were not supported by the general observance of the Sabbath,
and it was almost impossible for Daniel and his
companions to avoid apparent compliance with
idolatry, yet they refused to be cut off from Israel.
They cherished the law of Israel in their hearts,
they took it as the rule of their own lives, and thus
they were conscious of a Divine Presence reigning
within and of aspirations for the restoration of the
external acknowledgment of their God.

The devout men of the exile were exposed to
bitter trials, not only at the hands of their heathen
conquerors, to whom the fact that they had been
conquered seemed a proof of the inability of their
God to help, but more especially at the hands of
renegade Jews who were ready to adapt themselves
to their surroundings and mocked at the idealists
and their aspiration. The imprecatory psalms give
expression to the horror which was aroused by

those who were disloyal to the traditions of their race, and to the hope that such men might not survive to contaminate the people in time to come. There is evidence of the loyalty to Jehovah which inspired some of the exiles, and of which none of the accidents of time or place could deprive them.

The kindred spirits, who enjoyed this sense of God's will as reigning in their hearts, were not satisfied that He should be a private possession of their own, but were eager that the whole of the society in which they lived should be permeated by this devotion and should be a witness to the nations of the goodness of God. They desired to see the restoration of a Theocracy which should set forth the righteousness of God from Jerusalem as a centre, and where in organised worship there might be national response to the goodness of God.

22   Since the time of S. Paul a contrast has always been drawn between the legal and the spiritual in religion—the compliance with external maxims on the one hand, and the spontaneity of personal devotion on the other. But there was a phase in the religious development of Israel when the individual found, in the divine will for the community, the highest aim for his own personal life. The law was not merely a code to be enforced, it was the noblest expression of the divine ideal for man's life to which the devout man sought to conform. Many enthusiasts are carried away to-day by dreams of a Socialism which shall give the

greatest possible welfare to each individual; of some great enthusiasts for reconstructing our social system as a system, it has been said by intimate acquaintances that the wrongs and sufferings of individuals do not seem to appeal to their sympathies. In a somewhat similar way the enthusiasm for a Theocracy took a hold on prophets and devout men after the time of Josiah. They despaired of the decadent monarchy at Jerusalem, but saw a means of salvation for society and for themselves in accepting the divine revelation. This enthusiasm for the divine order as a rule for society and a guide for life is put before us in Deuteronomy vi. 1-7. "These are the commandments, the "statutes and the judgments which the Lord your "God commanded to teach you, that ye might do "them in the land whither `ye go to possess it. "That thou mightest fear the Lord thy God, to "keep all His statutes and His commandments "which I command thee, thou and thy son, and "thy son's son, all the days of thy life, and that "thy days may be prolonged."..."Thou shalt "love the Lord thy God with all thy soul and with "all thy might, and these words which I command "thee this day shall be in thy heart, and thou shalt "teach them diligently unto thy children, and "shalt talk of them when thou sittest in thy house, "and when thou walkest by the way and when thou "liest down and when thou risest up." God had revealed His Will to the Community; and to make

that Will the guide of their own personal lives was
the ambition of the men who had preserved their
patriotic faith. through the dark days of the exile,
and who hoped for the restoration of a true
Theocracy at Jerusalem. The 119th Psalm, when-
ever it was written, gives expression to this enthusiasm for God's revelation of His Will; its form
makes it a guide to memory, and it was written, not
as a song of praise, but in the hope that its recital
might be a devout exercise in recalling the help
and guidance which God had prepared for those
that love Him. The new Theocracy was not to be for
all time; it was bound sooner or later to show its
limitations and defects as an earthly expression of
God's eternal will; but it set forth a more personal
ideal than the monarchy had afforded, and came
home to devout men with·all the force of a personal
conviction[1].

It seems natural to assume that in such an elabo-
rate acrostic as Ps. cxix there is a systematic
arrangement of the subject matter[2], but careful
students have failed to detect the method the
psalmist has adopted[3], either in the composition as
a whole, or in the structure of the particular stanzas.
It seems not impossible to trace antiphonal arrangement, not only in the two members of each verse,

[1] W. Robertson Smith, *op. cit.* 177.
[2] Bishop C. Wordsworth, *Commentary on the Holy Bible.
Psalms*, cxix, p. 187.
[3] King, *The Psalms in Three Collections*, p. 52,

but also between each pair of verses, though this is not slavishly adhered to; and the psalm seems to open with personal aspiration (1–56), to address God Himself as the Giver of all good (57–112) and as giving guidance in all the conditions of life (113–176), but though it has been "a pattern of "devotion for all ages" it has some noticeable features which reflect the era when the thoughts it contains were a new inspiration.

The psalmist did not distinguish the ceremonial[1] from the moral law, and found a delight in fulfilling God's requirements in every way; but there is in the psalm wonderfully little specific allusion to external ordinances; or to the Temple or the City where sacrifices had been maintained and were re-established. The aspiration for single-hearted love of the will of God in the heart is so absorbing that very little reference is made to external conditions at all.

The consciousness of the privilege of having such knowledge revealed gives the psalmist a sense of the difference between the Theocracy and the heathen around, and a consciousness of rectitude as compared with them, which seem to show an inadequate recognition of the reality of personal guilt. The psalmist here is face to face with an

[1] The sense of obligation to punctilious observance of ceremonial becomes superstitious if it is regarded as a means of making "the gods subservient to the will of man," as it was among the ancient Romans. Döllinger, *The Gentile and the Jew*, II, 210.

embodiment of the Divine Will, rather than with the thought of the Eternal God Himself, as the prophets had been; he does not sound the depths that are revealed in the *De profundis*, and does not give expression to such a sense of guilt, or of the joy of forgiveness as we find in the utterances of many of the saints. Just as he does not realise the sense of sin as it has been felt in Christian times, so too we may notice the limitations of his devout hope; there are no hints of a life beyond the grave, or of the anticipation of a resurrection, which had become so generally diffused at the time of our Lord; the psalmist does not look beyond this earthly sphere, but is satisfied with the belief that all perplexities are solved by the light God has given.

23   The Israelites seem to have had a primitive belief in the continuance of a shadowy existence after death, but an existence where all the vigour of life had ceased, and where there was no longer a possibility of communion with God. They seem to have had no hopes of reward for the righteous in the world to come, nor fears for the punishment of the wicked personally, though they regarded the place of the dead as a refuge for those who had tasted most deeply of the sorrows of life (Job iii. 17). But there is little sign of hope for a personal resurrection such as the prophet cherished for national resurrection (Ezek. xxxvii). The name which the good man left behind him might be a most precious possession to his descendants, but he could not hope for continued life of his own, as

an inspiration to a strenuous life or to self-sacrifice.
The hope of a personal immortality and of a personal resurrection seems to have been gradually
diffused and to have rested on a sense of personal
communion with the Eternal God as something
which was not dependent on earthly conditions.
Just as the righteousness[1] of God gives its meaning
to human righteousness, so is participation in the
life of God the ground of the human hope of life
after death. The life of God is apart from the
limitations of place and time, and those who come
to enter into the wisdom of God have a share in His
undying life[2]. "He created all things that they
"might have their being, and the generations of
"the world were healthful; and there is no poison
"of destruction in them, nor the kingdom of death
"upon them." In the Wisdom literature we realise
how much the hope of immortality has come to be
the main motive of a godly life, and how the ungodly
being without God are without hope in the world.
"Our life is short and tedious and in the death of a
"man there is no remedy"..."we are born at all
"adventure, and we shall be hereafter as though
"we had never been, for the breath in our nostrils
"is as smoke and a little spark in the moving of our
"heart, which being extinguished our body shall be
"turned into ashes and our spirit shall vanish as
"the soft air." To those who reasoned thus it

[1] G. A. Smith, *Isaiah*, II, 224.
[2] *The 16th Psalm*, W. Robertson Smith, *The Expositor*
(1876), IV, 341 ff.

seemed that the way to make the most of life was
to enjoy the present, "let none of us go without
"his part in our voluptuousness, let us leave tokens
"of our joyfulness in every place" (Wisdom ii).
But the hope of immortality gave a new sense of
values in earthly life to those who cherished it.
"Every man that hath this hope set on Him," as
S. John said, "purifieth himself even as He is pure."
"God is not the God of the dead, but of the living."
The kindred spirits who had come to realise that
communion with God was not broken by death,
and believed that God had created man to be
immortal and to be an image of His own eternity,
were able to look at death with new eyes. "The
"souls of the righteous are in the hand of God, and
"there shall no torment touch them. In the sight
"of the unwise they seem to die, and their depar-
"ture is taken for misery, and their going from us
"to be utter destruction but they are in peace."
The hope of immortality has come, in Christian
times, to be regarded as an essential element in
religion, and its absence as a sign of Atheism; but
this hope was a comparatively late development,
and seems to have grown up and developed in the
new Theocracy. The story of the reconstruction of
the Jewish nation, in spite of the exile and dispersion, and of the religious institutions at Jerusalem,
is of peculiar interest to Christians, as it helps us
to understand the conditions under which our Lord
lived and taught, and the genesis of the Christian
Church.

VII

THE NEW THEOCRACY

24 The character of the new Theocracy was greatly affected by the conditions under which this National Self-consciousness came into being. There were kindred spirits among the captives who deeply prized the will of God as it was revealed to them in the Law, and cultivated the love of the Law in their own hearts, but were not satisfied to treasure their communion with God as a private possession. They longed to create a godly society which should be a witness to the world of the truths that had come home to their own souls. They could not be contented to settle down in the lands to which they had been transplanted; their hearts yearned for a restoration to their own land, and they looked for it as a sign that God had at length punished the backslidings of His people, and that He was willing that they should have the opportunity of once more enjoying the prosperity which they had forfeited by their disobedience. "Then they that feared the Lord "spake often one to another"; they set themselves to restore the ancient city, and the ancient worship as a witness which the world could appreciate of

the living power of the God to whom they were devoted in their hearts.

The old Theocracy had been a realm, where the maintenance of the hereditary succession in David's line, and the prosperity of the people had been taken as the marks of divine favour. But the restored Theocracy was different in character; there was no longer a King with his court, and national worship could not be re-established under royal patronage. The hope of a conquering Messiah was relegated to a distant future, and the religious needs of the present were met by the creation of a society in which the divine law should be enforced, as it never had been in the old days. The new Theocracy is often spoken of as a " Jewish Church" in contradistinction to the "Realm" round which the religious life of Israel had hitherto centred.

Ezra seems to have been the leading spirit in shaping this movement, and his account of it indicates the main features. The Lord stirred up the spirit of Cyrus, King of Persia, who proclaimed throughout his dominions, "The Lord God of "heaven hath given me all the kingdoms of the "earth, and He hath charged me to build Him a "house at Jerusalem which is in Judah. Who is "there among you of all His people? His God be "with him and let him go up to Jerusalem and "build the house of the Lord God of Israel...and "whoso remaineth in any place where he sojourneth "let the men of his place help him with silver and

"with gold and with goods and with beasts, beside
"the freewill offering for the house of God that is
"in Jerusalem." There was a response to this
proclamation which seemed as memorable as the
deliverance from Egypt had been: "Then rose up
"the chief of the fathers of Judah and Benjamin
"and the priests and the Levites, with all them
"whose spirit God had raised, to go up to build the
"house of the Lord" (Ezra i. 1–7). He has given
us a long catalogue of the names of those who were
thus gathered together out of the districts in which
they had settled, to start on their long pilgrimage,
and to institute a new Theocracy in the place which
had such sacred associations. We have little
information regarding the assignment of land to
the captives who returned, but the silence suggests
that this was done under the authority of Cyrus
(Nehemiah v. 3) and that it was not till the time of
Nehemiah that civil affairs were directed by a
Jewish Governor. The restored Jerusalem was not
an independent polity with a distinct life of its
own, but was dependent upon foreign powers, and
its politics were chiefly concerned with efforts to
obtain favourable consideration from these powers
rather than with attempts to pursue national aims
of its own.

The great distinction of this new Theocracy from
the old,—of this "gathered church," from the
realm that had been conquered—was its greater
exclusiveness. The leaders were nervously anxious

that the restored city should not be contaminated by any alien rites such as Solomon had permitted, or suffer by any laxity. The pilgrims refused the aid which was proffered by the people of the land who professed to seek the same God; the enmity of these adversaries was roused by the rejection of their offers (Ezra iv. 3) and they succeeded in stopping the work for a time. But the laxity which prevailed among some of the restored people also needed to be corrected. Ezra recounts how "The "princes came to me saying, The people of Israel, "the priests and the Levites have not separated "themselves from the people of the lands, but have "taken of their daughters for themselves and for "their sons, so that the holy seed have mingled "themselves with the people of those lands, yea, "the hand of the princes and rulers hath been chief "in this trespass." Ezra found himself face to face with the laxity which had called down divine displeasure in the days gone by, and there assembled with him every one that trembled at the words of the God of Israel (Ezra ix. 4); the community was purged of this trespass and entered into a resolution to maintain the purity of their race, and the strict regularity of their homage to the God who had not only delivered them from Egypt but gathered them from foreign lands.

The new Theocracy was formed by men who feared the Lord, and desired to serve Him in purity; it thus had a character of finality and exclusiveness, and imposed limitations which the Christian Church has outgrown. The Jewish Theocracy was organised by saints who desired to maintain their separatism from evil surroundings, and who believed they had a complete revelation of God's Will for man in the Law; their mission was to maintain this testimony in its purity; and the institutions were formed and maintained by those who had this Law in their hearts and who were eager to bring others up to their standard. They had not attained to the conception of God's revelation as progressive,—of the work of the Church in awakening the conscience, and forming the individual mind and stimulating to nobler aspirations, and of her vocation as having a mission to the world and a power of regenerating every individual. It was S. Paul who realised the possibilities of progress which the gospel afforded, and which the Judaism in which he had been brought up did not offer. There has always been a temptation for Christian men to fall back upon the exclusiveness of a Theocracy, as formed by good men, and to forget the power of Christ to appeal to sinful men everywhere and transform them by the renewing of their minds. They have been convinced that the maintenance of godly society reacts upon the formation of personal character. But the creation of a godly society does not mechanically produce the highest type of personal character, though it may diffuse and perpetuate conditions which favour

it, and render a high level of character attainable
by ordinary men who take their tone from their
surroundings. Ezra and his successors did succeed
in creating a godly society; but the Theocracy they
valued so highly failed to mould characters that
had spontaneity and transparency and strenuous-
ness.

25   The determined effort to enforce and main-
     tain this exclusive character was the funda-
mental difference between the new Theocracy and
the old. There were other contrasts however. The
ancient realm had been a territory with complete
political independence, while the privileges of the
new Theocracy rested on the concessions granted
by Cyrus; though the people lived under the rule
of their own princes and Sanhedrin there was no
territorial sovereignty. The Maccabees asserted
their independence for a time, but under Persian,
Greek and Roman Rule, the Aristocracy at Jerusalem were rather concerned to avoid causes of
possible conflict than to cherish political and
patriotic aims; the Sadducees seem on the whole
to have cultivated the wisdom of political opportunists. Jerusalem at the time of our Lord was
analogous to a City State; and the Jews who were
scattered throughout the world lived by Jewish
Law, just as the Roman citizen was a privileged
person in all the lands of the Roman Empire. The
old Theocracy had been founded among a nomadic
people, and after they settled in Canaan the traces

of patriarchal and communal possession long remained; but Palestine had passed into a much more
advanced condition economically; and opportunities of commercial intercourse had reacted on the
constitution of society; little attempt was made
under the new Theocracy to subordinate economic
conditions to common political aims; it seems as
if their common religious history and faith and
participation in national worship and obedience to
the divine Law were the only things that held the
people together.

A much clearer sense of personal duty to God
was diffused under the new Theocracy than under
the old. In the old days Israelites believed that
the triumph of God was exhibited by the prosperity
and successes of His people; under the new regime
they felt that it had become incumbent on His
chosen to set forth the character of God by holiness
as a society. Men had feared in the old days to be
cut off from Israel, and from sharing in the prosperity which God had promised to His people; but
the responsibility for pleasing God and keeping
His covenant rather lay with those who ruled, with
kings and priests, than with the people. It was
generally recognised that the new society could not
be itself a witness for God if it was disfigured by
open evil, and there was a sense of sin as a scandal,
and of the shamefulness of sin as a failure to live
up to the standard of society, which does not
appear to have been diffused in the old realm. This

is not adequate from the Christian standpoint, for it measures evil by its bearing on human society, and not by its heinousness in the sight of God, as is done in Ps. li. 4; but still it marks a phase of religion. Daniel portrays the awakening to universal contempt as the horror of the final judgment on evil; indulgence in unhallowed rites was felt to be a scandal in a God-fearing community; but a deeper sense of guilt in the sight of God was at length wakened among the people generally, when S. John the Baptist's preaching called them to try and see themselves as they were in His sight.

26   The basis of the new Theocracy lay, not in a line of independent monarchs, but in the Law, which gave expression to the national institutions; the desire to understand better the Will of God as He had revealed it, and to make this the rule of personal life and of lives associated in society, dominated the whole of this new Theocracy. Ezra was the first of the scribes who devoted themselves to the minute study and exposition of the Law; the organisation of the regular assemblies in synagogues for the reading of the Law, and for instruction in it cannot be before his date[1]. The worship which he instituted took the place of the local sacrifices which had been maintained under the old realm, and national worship was concen-

---

[1] I. Abrahams (*Pharisaism and the Gospels*, p. 1) argues against the opinion that the Palestine synagogues were organised after the time of the Maccabees.

trated in Jerusalem where the sacrifices were carried on by a priestly caste in strict accordance with the restored Law. There seems to have been some special arrangement in Alexandria, but on the whole it is true to say that the pious Jew, whether in the Holy Land itself or among those dispersed in heathen countries, used his opportunities for making the Law the rule of his life, and only occasionally participated personally in the sacrifices at Jerusalem which were felt to be a bond of union holding the whole nation together.

The dangers of such a society, requiring obedience to a code for personal life, lay in the fact that effort was so much directed at setting a good example, and maintaining external correctness. The Pharisees in particular were devoted to the minute observance of the Law, and enjoyed a reputation of being separated from the nation at large by the pains they took in the duties of religion, and especially in the giving of alms. There is a constant danger for pious men to think habitually of their influence on others and to be actuated by the desire of setting a good example so that the denunciations of our Lord against the exclusiveness of the Pharisees are a needed warning which is never out of date.

This habit of cultivating external compliance, and thus setting forth the Divine Will for mankind, had its natural result in the superciliousness of the Pharisees towards those of their race who were

content with a lower standard than their own.
"This people which knoweth not the Law is
"cursed." The attempt to insist on the more complete observance of the Law especially in regard to
that distinctively national institution—the Sabbath
—is brought constantly before us in the gospels.
By public censures, and by cutting off from the
synagogues, the rulers were able to bring very
strong pressure to bear; they fell into the blunder,
which has beset so many legalists, of trying to
exalt the authority of the Law they enforced by
exaggerating its antiquity. The gradual growth of
a clearer consciousness of God and of His education
of the chosen race has been obscured by the
desire of the scribes to read back the exclusiveness
which characterised the new Theocracy into the
times of the old realm. Though God is unchanging,
the human apprehension of Him and of His Will
has changed under His guidance; He is not really
honoured by efforts to represent the spiritual consciousness as identical in all ages, or to read the
story of the past in the light of later conceptions
of religious duty.

The enthusiasm for God's Law and the belief in
its finality also affected the Jews' conception of
other nations, and their hopes for the future.
The belief in God as ruling over all mankind, and
not merely as a national God, involved the expectation that all nations would be led to recognise
and to live by the divine Law. There was a constant

effort for "peaceful penetration" by the Jews in
foreign lands, who compassed sea and land to make
one proselyte; they also cherished the hope of a
Messiah, who would come to be the divine instrument for enforcing God's Judgments throughout
the world. Jerusalem was the centre from which
judgment would go forth, and Jerusalem was the
centre at which the peoples of the world would be
arraigned; this expectation of a Messiah as judge,
gave a new form to the belief in a continued royal
succession, and to the conception of the destiny of
the chosen people.

27   The observance of the Law came to be
        thought of as a national testimony to the
world, and the maintenance of worship at Jerusalem
was regarded as the condition of national acceptance with God. Ezekiel had given expression to
the hopes which cheered the captives, "Now will I
"bring again the captivity of Jacob, and have
"mercy upon the whole house of Israel and will be
"jealous for my holy name; after that they have
"borne their shame, and all their trespasses where-
"with they have trespassed against me when they
"dwelt safely in their land and none made them
"afraid. When I have brought them again from the
"people, and gathered them out of their enemies'
"lands, and am sanctified in them in the sight of
"many nations; then shall they know that I am
"the Lord their God which caused them to be led
"into captivity among the heathen; but I have

"gathered them into their own land and have left
"none of them any more there; neither will I hide
"my face any more from them, for I have poured
"out my spirit upon the house of Israel, saith the
"Lord God" (Ezek. xxxix.25-29). The great achieve-
ment to which he looked forward was the rebuilding
of the Temple, on a hallowed site where it should no
longer be defiled by the carcases of their kings
(Ezek. xliii. 9), and where God would "dwell in
"the midst of them for ever." The maintenance of
national worship had been an ideal of the prophet;
its interruption by Antiochus Epiphanes was an
affliction which left an indelible impression on the
people, and deepened their attachment to the
Temple which was purged and restored with increased magnificence. The throes which marked
the final destruction of Jerusalem showed at once
the determination of the Jewish people to preserve
this centre of national worship, and the determination of the Romans to do away with this centre of
disaffection to imperial organisation[1].

[1] The Roman generals according to Josephus, *B. J.* vi,
cap. iii, were reluctant "to burn down such a vast work
"which would be an ornament to the Roman govern-
"ment while it continued,"—and would have desired to
preserve it, if they could root out its religious associations.
Titus, according to the sentences attributed to Tacitus
(Church and Brodribb, *History of Tacitus*, p. xv), was
"of opinion that the Temple more than anything else must
"be destroyed, that so the Jewish and the Christian super-
"stitions might be thoroughly eradicated. These supersti-
"tions, though mutually opposed, had had their origin in the

The enthusiasm for this Theocracy and the continuance of national worship was compatible with an inadequate care for personal religion. The maintenance of a saintly life of detachment from things sensual was indeed the object of the Essenes, in their retirement from the world, but they aimed at avoidance of evil, and seem to have had little sense of need for personal repentance from evil within. There was an overvaluation of sacred places and sacred things and an inadequate recognition of the measures of spiritual reality. Whosoever "shall swear by the Temple, sweareth by it and "by him that dwelleth therein" (S. Matt. xxiii. 21). In spite of all that was done by this Theocracy, and by religious society, it neither gave opportunity for the growth of the spiritual consciousness of a nation on all its sides, nor for the development of the personal religious consciousness of men individually.

"same people; the Christians had risen up from among the "Jews; if the root was removed, the stem would soon perish." The persistence of the Jews rendered it inevitable that the Romans should destroy the Temple at Jerusalem, and close the recently established temple at Heliopolis; after the rebellion of Bar Cochba, Hadrian founded Aelia on the site of Jerusalem, and set himself to stamp out the national rites and institutions of the Jews.

VIII

THE PERSON OF CHRIST

28 The revelation of the character of God which was given in the person of our Lord Jesus Christ transcends all previous experience. His consciousness of God, and the expression in His Words and Deeds of this conscious desire to realise God's Will, sum up and complete all the knowledge of God that had come in the experience of the chosen people; as Kings, or Priests or Prophets. It took shape not merely in a national but in a personal life. We are fortunate in having records, not only of the impression it made at first, but of the fuller appreciation of those who on reflection were better able to grasp its real significance. The synoptic Gospels reflect the witness which was borne by the Apostles, when they went forth, after the first Whitsunday to discharge the commission they had received to preach and baptise; while the Epistles of S. Paul and the Gospel of S. John embody the experience of divine power which had come home to them in these first days.

By His preaching in Galilee Christ had appealed to the expectation of a new era of the manifestation of divine power, and He was hailed as a prophet. He spake with authority, as the prophets were able to do because of their intimacy with God Himself, and not merely as a learned expounder of God's written word. He claimed not only to be so intimate with God as to be acquainted with His purpose, but to have inherent powers which the prophets did not possess; He was conscious of Sonship; at His Baptism a voice had come from heaven confirming the claim that He was the beloved Son. He exercised divine power personally in forgiving the sins of the man who was palsied; and by the signs He showed in casting out devils, in ruling the waves, and in His miracles of healing, He convinced many of His followers of the reality of the divine power which He claimed. His consciousness of Sonship enabled Him to proclaim the truth as to the relation of God and Man, and to declare that God had a personal care for each individual. The prophets of old had, generally speaking, had a divine message for the nation[1], but Christ preached the gospel that the great God was ready to bestow fatherly care on every man personally and individually; this was the gospel which the disciples were sent forth to declare in Galilee.

The declaration of God's fatherly personal care over every one of His children must have been most welcome to those who had been awakened to a sense of their personal sin by the preaching of

---

[1] Jeremiah is remarkable however for his "vindication "of individuality" (G. A. Smith, *Isaiah*, II, 41) and Ezekiel's teaching is similar (cf. Ezek. xviii. 4).

S. John the Baptist. He had roused them from satisfaction with their privileges of citizenship, and their external compliance with a divine Law, to a sense of their personal unworthiness in the eyes of the Holy God, whose kingdom was at hand. Our Lord's consciousness of Sonship, and declaration of the Fatherhood of God, came as deliverance to those who were oppressed by the burden of sin, and also opened up a vista as to the standard at which they ought to aim. In the Sermon on the Mount Christ declares the inadequacy of the Law by which they had shaped their lives, and announces the need of an inner devotion that exceeds the righteousness of the Scribes and Pharisees. "Be ye "therefore perfect, even as your Father in Heaven "is perfect." The call to the constant service of man is also put strongly by Christ in speaking of Himself as a brother and by appeals to the duty of seeing Him in any human sufferer. His teaching is far deeper than that of the Scribes, since He insists on personal devotion as primary and fundamental, not merely as a condition of good citizenship in a Theocracy.

Though much in the Galilaean preaching was very different from the teaching of the Scribes, and much was implicitly inconsistent with it, no open breach was made at first with the habits of thought and expectation that had come down by long tradition. Our Lord recognised the authority of the rulers, though He condemned the manner in

which they exercised that authority, and especially
criticised the restrictions they enforced in regard
to ceremonial cleanliness and the observance of the
Sabbath. But when His claim to be the Messiah
was publicly made by His solemn entry into
Jerusalem and by His assumption of authority in
His Father's house, the rulers took up the challenge.
He had, as was His habit, expounded more fully
to His disciples, the truth which had inspired His
public action; He told them of the Judgment to
come, and of the great work they expected the
Messiah to do; but this, as He conceived, was not so
much a judgment to be executed on all nations, as
on the persons small and great who should be
arraigned before Him, and who would be judged
for the deeds done in the body. The judgment was
thought of as extraordinarily exacting; it was not
so much breaches of the Law that He would condemn as the neglect of opportunities. There was
need for His disciples to be unwearied in well doing
if they were to escape His condemnation.

His claim to divine authority seemed to be dis-
proved once for all, when He was taken by the
rulers to be crucified, and buried, but it was
revived with fresh conviction by the disciples at
His Resurrection. Even in all He had gone through
they recognised new reasons for accepting Him,
for under His guidance the disciples at Emmaus
found the prophetic foreshadowing of a suffering
Messiah. Finally in the gift of Whitsunday they

recognised that Joel's expectation of the diffusion of the prophetic intimacy with God, had been realised. The acceptance of Christ as Messiah, as witnessed by His Resurrection, supplemented all they had been taught as Jews to reverence, by giving it a deeper meaning, and rousing a new inspiration. Through Him they learned to be conscious of Sonship with God themselves, and of the desire to fulfil the Heavenly Father's Will.

29   The Apostles went forth as missionaries to their own people, beginning at Jerusalem, and so long as their preaching was addressed to the Jews who lived in the land where the message of S. John the Baptist had made such an impression, and in which pious Jews assembled for the great feasts, the gospel of Christ which they preached was compatible with the observance of the national ordinances. The gospel was a personal message of personal salvation through the power of Christ, and did not necessarily raise any questions as to the maintenance of the traditional ordinances. Though S. Peter was impelled to accept Cornelius and his family as Christians, who had been moved to repentance by the Spirit of God, he seems to have regarded their case as exceptional. It was only when the missionary work of the Church was extended by S. Paul and S. Barnabas and reached the Gentile population of heathen cities that difficulties arose as to the permanent and normal requirements of the Christian life. The observance

of the ordinances in regard to clean and unclean meats, and in regard to circumcision and the Sabbath had been the characteristic features that divided the people of God from the heathen around them, and the question now arose, in regard to Gentile Christians, whether the maintenance of these ordinances was essential or not. The Council at Jerusalem attempted a compromise, and did not insist on the strict observance by Gentile Christians of the rules in regard to what was common and unclean (Acts xv. 20, 21) or in regard to circumcision and the Sabbath; while S. Paul in his preaching insisted on the inadequacy of the external compliance which the Law demanded (Acts xiii. 39), and on the power of faith in Christ to work for righteousness in the heart and life. Even S. Peter is represented as accepting a very similar view in regard to the Law (Acts xv. 10, 11); and the decision thus obtained had far-reaching practical consequences, since it gave rise to confusion in Jewish communities. The observance of this Law had been the badge of the Jewish communities in every city, and the heresy of the sect of Nazarenes who held that the effort to maintain the Mosaic ordinances was unnecessary, seemed to strike at that which had rendered Judaism a witness for God to an evil world. The men who had lived and suffered in this faith could not tamely acquiesce in the teaching of the Christian missionaries[1] that the witness of

[1] The *Epistle of S. Barnabas* condemns the Jews for

Judaism was now superseded; since Christ had given a pledge in the Resurrection of His power to forgive sins (1 Cor. xv. 17), and had created a people of God bound together, not by the observance of new ordinances, but by oneness with Him, to witness for Him by their lives.

The commission to preach in Gentile cities had led to the breaking out of a controversy which caused dissension in every community of the Jewish world; it roused a criticism against the narrowness of the Jewish Law, and the attempt to confine the enjoyment of God's favour to the men who observed the customs of a particular race. In the *Acts of the Apostles* we can follow the difficulties which arose in one city after another, and additional evidence is furnished by the themes which recur in S. Paul's Epistles.

30   The Temple at Jerusalem had been a rallying point; and participation in the sacrifices there had been regarded as a privilege which was distinctive of the whole of the Jewish people scattered throughout the world; any intrusion into this sanctuary was jealously guarded against. S. Paul valued this religious privilege himself; but he made no attempt to obtain it for the Gentile Christians, though the suspicion that he had done so roused the men of Jerusalem to plot his death. The centre of the spiritual life of the

observing the ancient ordinances literally and failing to apprehend their spiritual sense.

Christians, both Jew and Gentile, could not be found in an earthly city or by participation in the sacrifices of an earthly temple, since they looked to a Heavenly Jerusalem and a Temple not made with hands, where, as the *Epistle to the Hebrews* declares, a Great High Priest ever liveth to make intercession for us. The thought of Christ as Himself a sacrifice, as one who had made atonement on the cross for the sins of the whole world, superseded the belief that the ceremonies of the day of Atonement made satisfaction for the sins of the nation,—of all who claimed the right to participate in the paschal feast. Christ by His Sacrifice of Himself had done away with the need of earthly sacrifices to take away the burden and shame of sin, and cleanse the conscience, and thus the centre of the spiritual life of the dispersed people of God was transferred; it was no longer thought of as an earthly city, with its conditions of citizenship, but as an Eternal High Priest in a Heavenly Temple. Jerusalem which is above is free.

31   There was in the apostolic age a revolution in the spiritual consciousness, far and wide; and this experience of the power of Christ in the world, threw on His own life and purpose a new light, which even those who were most closely associated with Him had failed to appreciate at first. The *Gospel according to S. John* professes to give this fuller apprehension of Christ's person which came to the apostles, but only in retrospect. They

did not appreciate the meaning of His words in regard to the destruction of the Temple, till they realised that He spake of the temple of His body. "When therefore He was risen from the dead, His "disciples remembered that He had said this unto "them; and they believed the Scripture and the "word which Jesus had said" (S. John ii. 21, 22). It was so too, that they saw the significance of His claim to be the King of the Jews: "These things "understood not His disciples at the first; but when "Jesus was glorified, then remembered they that "these things were written of Him, and that they "had done these things unto Him" (S. John xii. 16, see also xiii. 7). It cannot be a matter of surprise that this later gospel records important incidents which the earlier writers, with their minds fixed on the preaching in Galilee, had passed over in silence. The signs of ever increasing suspicion and hostility on the part of the leaders of the Jews are carefully noted, as their full significance had at last become apparent; and the teaching of our Lord, as it was given to the inner circle of His friends and as it concerned Himself and His aims, is carefully recorded, while the other gospels are on the whole content to put on record His sayings in public.

32   Along with this fuller appreciation of Christ in His earthly life, there is also a different apprehension of the work which He committed to His apostles to carry on. There was and is need for missionary activity,—for preaching and baptising;

but S. John also records the charge to S. Peter, which tells of pastoral responsibility for the cure of souls. Feed my lambs; feed my sheep; feed my sheep (S. John xxi. 15–17). In this gospel too we get our Lord's own account of the significance of the miraculous feeding of the multitude as a pledge of His power to nourish the spiritual life by the sacrament of His body and blood (S. John vi). This later phase of the Christian life of the apostolic age is reflected in S. Paul's pastoral epistles, where we feel his responsibility for the care of all the churches, and for the maintenance of the ordinances which were to keep alive in all ages and in all places the memory of Christ—of that which He had been and is eternally. As the Apostles were removed one by one their places were taken in one community after another by episcopoi who were responsible for the cure of the souls in their charge, for intercommunication with other churches[1], and for passing on to other generations the truth they had received.

33   The Resurrection of our Lord was the great subject of the missionary preaching of the apostles, but they did not content themselves with the announcement of the bare fact; they were eager that others should feel for themselves the power of the Resurrection. Our Lord had realised His relations with God and Man as none had ever done before; "all power is given me in heaven and in "earth." He did not indeed claim to have a perfectly

[1] W. M. Ramsay, *The Church in the Roman Empire*, 366.

complete knowledge or to enable His disciples to foresee the future in all its details, but to give them strength and guidance to lead their own lives and to follow Him. This power of an endless life must be maintained as a conscious possession; and the consciousness of divine power as breaking the bonds of sin within gave force to the conviction of our Lord's triumph in breaking the power of death. The Resurrection had been a pledge of the Divine Power that is living for ever, and those who learn to rely upon it are delivered from the fear of demons and of death, from the sense of remorse and shame of sin, and from carelessness and vacillation of purpose so as to be able to make the most of their lives. The apostles had felt this themselves, and they wished others to feel it too; the joyfulness of their lives, their hopefulness and unselfishness were the best utterance of the conviction that had been a power in their own lives; but there was also need to put this conviction in words, and to find the best words for telling of the living power of which they were conscious. The desire to communicate and perpetuate the knowledge that had come to them as a revelation gave rise to a sense of the need and importance of proper expression; much of the difficulty of the apostles, as of missionaries to-day, arose from the lack of spirituality among their hearers. These men lived on too low a level, they had such a gross view of the gods and such an inadequate view of the possibilities of human life, that it was not easy to find language in which to express the unique power of Christ to men who were content to rely on the exercise of other and lesser powers on their behalf, and to live their lives in a dimmer light.

Even for the Jew, with his enthusiasm for a religious nation and for living in accordance with its customs, there was need of a revolution if he were to come under a sense of the power of a personal saviour from personal sin; the links of connection were of the closest, but the change in the attitude towards life was immeasurable. Still greater was the task which S. Paul set himself in preaching to the Gentile world. "Whom therefore "ye ignorantly worship, Him declare I unto you" (Acts xvii. 23). The difficulty was all the greater because it was the aim of the apostles to complete imperfect knowledge, and to build upon what their hearers recognised as true. S. Paul was all things to all men, because he hoped, by making the most of the religious truth to which they had already attained, to lead them to appreciate the revelation of God in the person of Jesus Christ.

As we look back we can see how immensely the experience of something like two millenniums had given definiteness to the religious consciousness of Man. Abraham had cherished a vague confidence in Some One who was reliable amid all the unintelligibleness of the world and the arbitrariness of human kind; but his sense of the presence of this reliable friend was only occasional, his expectation of the prospect held out to him was curiously dim. He could but grope after God if haply he might find Him. But the gospel held out a knowledge of Christ as an ever present help, through whom man could depend on the constant care of the Heavenly Father, who was willing to take on Himself the burden of sin committed, and to bestow His own insight and persistence in doing the Will of God. While there had been this wonderful advance in the definiteness of the knowledge of God, as near us and as loving us, there was also a far fuller sense of the nature of Man, and the possibilities that lay before him. "What is Man," the Psalmist had asked, "that Thou art mindful of Him?"; but it was not till our Lord took our nature upon Him that the possibilities of human life were fully revealed, and the infinite value of personal human life in the sight of God. In becoming conscious of his oneness with Christ, each man might become conscious of his true dignity and learn to make the most of his own life. The apostles knew that Christ could do this, for they knew He had done it for them, and numberless converts had confirmed the truth in their own experience.

S. Paul, like other Christian missionaries, could not but recognise a partial truth in other religions, because it was his claim that the faith of Christ superseded them; Greeks had perceived the fatherhood of God, for "we are also His offspring"; and the Law had been a "schoolmaster to lead him to

"Christ." But it was his mission to help men to attain to the apprehension of all that had been implied in the religious consciousness in bygone days, by striving to enter into and be one with the mind of Christ Jesus.

The contact with other religions forced the men of the sub-apostolic ages to endeavour to find language in which to convey their sense of the meaning of the facts to which they bore witness, and of the ordinances which they introduced and maintained. They were also forced to explain where other religions seemed to them lacking in spiritual power, and inadequate or unsatisfying— to show how Judaism and heathenism were incomplete, and could never save the conscience from the sense of sin. The controversies, in which the apologists engaged, necessarily turned on the defectiveness of the religions which Christians regarded as superseded; Gnosticism accentuated the resemblances with other religions, and Arianism presented Christianity in a form in which its distinctiveness, and its unique powers of regenerating the inner man were disguised and allowed to drop out of sight.

The controversies of the first ages were not mere logomachies, they had an immense practical importance for their own age in formulating for thought the spiritual power which was working among men, and in perpetuating to coming generations a knowledge of the powers which can regenerate mankind.

IX

CHRISTENDOM

I. THE FOUNDATION

34 In His personal life Christ gathered through His own experience the different phases of spiritual consciousness which had been felt by all the Holy Men of old; in Him they are completed. But while all previous ages led up towards Him, the succeeding eras have looked back on Him as they do on no other human life; for by men in every age He has been regarded as a perfect human character, who passed through human life without defect, and who serves as a model for every age. His unique example has been reverenced by Christians; and many men of other faiths, or of none, have recognised in Him the very ideal of what a human life should be. Those who have refused their admiration have either regarded Him as a mere idealist who was unfitted for an actual world, or have cherished some special ideal of society for which His character was not adapted. Celsus had such an enthusiasm for Roman Civilisation that he could only treat Him with contempt[1]; the followers of Nietzsche in the present day have

[1] T. R. Glover, *Conflict*, 249.

no use for such a weakling; and those, who regard
Militarism or Mammonism as the essential for the
lasting good of Society, cannot but condemn one
who discarded all their ideals. Even while we
recognise that there are some to whom Christ's life
does not appeal, we feel there is no other human
life that has won such wide and long continued
acceptance as a model and an example.

There are three great religious divisions of
Mankind: — Buddhism, Mohammedanism and
Christendom; though the followers of Buddha and
of Mohammed reverence them, they do not regard
these men as unique examples for personal life, as
Christ is revered in Christendom. Even if we take
Christendom in its widest sense, as the area in
which professing Christians exercise a dominating
influence, we may feel that this merely nominally
Christian society has distinctive features, and that
there is a recognition of the possibility of improvement which we do not find in Buddhism, and
a recognition of the possibilities of human life which
goes above and beyond the material paradise which
the Arabian prophet held out to his followers.

While these broad differences are apparent, there
is great difficulty in making any accurate comparison between such widely diffused and long continued
social systems. We have perhaps the best opportunity of setting the problem in a form in which it
can be intelligently discussed, if we remember that
each individual is to a great extent the product of

the environment in which he has been brought up. No personal life can be entirely isolated, or unaffected by its surroundings; and in the highest type of personal life which it produces, we have a test by which we can gauge the best of which any given society was capable. Marcus Aurelius may be accepted as a "saint of agnosticism"[1]; however much we admire him, we can see in his personality defects which reflect the ineffectiveness of Stoicism, and the crushing tyranny that characterised the Roman Empire at its best. A society shows its strength or its weakness as a living thing, not so much in great resources as in the type of personality it tends to produce. It is on this ground that the claims of Christendom to be a better system than Buddhism or Mohammedanism are to be rested.

When we cease to make these comparisons, and fix our attention on Christendom itself, the application of this standard seems to condemn all Christian institutions as failures. There is an extraordinary contrast between the life of Christ, and the lives of His professing followers. Even though we recognise that no society can perpetuate in all its members the full inspiration and aspiration which marks pioneers as great leaders, we cannot but feel that the gospel narratives show an unselfishness and a strenuous devotion to service which are in

---

[1] Coleridge, *Aids to Reflection*, (7th ed. 1854), 65.

striking contrast to the self-seeking and easy-going lives of so many of His professed followers.

Many of those, who feel this failure of Christian institutions most keenly and point it out most unflinchingly, recognise that the ideal of personal life and of social life, which is put forward in Christ's name, is wholly excellent if it could be realised; but they complain that it never has been realised and that it never can be. This habit of mind is perilously near to the pessimism which despairs of any permanent improvement, and is content to drift through life without much effort or purpose. It is sometimes content to concentrate attention on some limited aim, such as making the most of the individual in the hope that society will come right of itself, or on recasting of society as a means of moulding individual lives. Such attempts to simplify the problem fail to recognise that the reaction of society and the individual on each other is not merely mechanical, and that conscious effort is needed to effect improvements in society or to bring about the elevation of personal character. If we are content to let things drift, there is a danger of condoning the anarchy in which society ceases to exist as an organised community, or of apologising for the tyranny which stamps out all individual initiative.

The sense of the failure of Christian institutions may be made an excuse for lassitude and despair; but it may also be a stimulus to more thoughtful

and energetic action, and a call to perseverance.
To recognise that Christian institutions have failed
to produce a type of character that closely resembles
the character of Christ need not be to acquiesce in
that failure. The failure has not been absolute;
Christian ideals diffused themselves through society;
they did away with slavery and fostered chivalry;
later Christianity was an advance on the Roman
Empire, and has left a heritage to modern society.
In the eighteenth century there was an awaking of
Christian philanthropy which is not likely to be
wholly lost; and these gains are not merely in
society, they have been exemplified in numberless
personal lives. The failure of Christianity is well
worth taking to heart; those of us, who are not
supine and callous, will be ready to learn, as we do
from other failures, how we may discharge our task
better and be better able to foster individual lives
that are more unselfish and more strenuous.

35 When the authorities and the public realised
that the Christians formed a sect which was
distinct from Judaism, it almost appeared as if this
third race[1] had affinities with the Roman Empire in
their freedom from various characteristics which
rendered the Jews offensive to the population of
heathen cities. The exclusiveness of the Jews, and
their air of superciliousness in maintaining their
own ordinances, marked them out from their
neighbours. The Christians laid no stress on the

[1] Harnack, *Expansion of Christianity*, I, 336.

requirements· of the Jewish Law or the acceptance
of Jewish rites; but like the Empire they were
ready to accept men of any race as citizens and
members. It is possible that, from the very first,
S. Paul anticipated a time when Christianity would
become the religion of the Empire[1], but there were
to be long centuries of persecution and antagonism
before that result was attained. In the apostolic
age the chief difficulty arose from the antagonism
of the Jews, and from their readiness to accuse the
Christians of creating disturbances. The Roman
governors appear on the whole to have wished to
keep from interference when they could; but three
causes seemed to call for their intervention. The
preaching of Christ might interfere with the business of certain traders, as Demetrius complained at
Ephesus, or reduce the gains from soothsaying at
Philippi. The progress of Christianity might also
interfere with the institutions of society; there
was a difficulty about slavery which called forth
S. Paul's *Epistle to Philemon*; and new problems
were raised in regard to family life on which S. Paul
gave advice to the Corinthians; they appear in a
concrete form in the primitive element in the *Acts
of S. Paul and Thekla*[2]. The Roman Empire was
concerned to deal with cases of proved disorder;
the popular feeling which blamed the Christians
for creating disturbance could look for support

---

[1] W. M. Ramsay, *op. cit.* 148.
[2] *Op. cit.* 410.

from Roman officials. Mommsen assures us that the "persecution of the Christians was a standing "matter" like that of robbers[1]. The support of the magistrates could in all probability be counted upon more readily by their enemies, since Nero had treated the Christians as responsible for the burning of Rome; and the *First Epistle of S. Peter* and the *Apocalypse* of S. John, give evidence of a conscious antagonism between the Empire and the Christians. The cultivating of the habits of a good citizen[2] must have seemed to some Christians to be a tedious method of living down this antagonism, since the whole administrative machinery of the Empire had been directed against them by the caprice of Nero, and the arbitrary will which controlled the fabric of society. Through successive reigns the Christian was punishable by death, as being a danger to society; but there were changes from time to time, according as proof was required of some overt act which was detrimental to society[3], and according as there was more or less activity in searching out Christians under one Emperor or another.

The worship of the Emperor, as supreme in the affairs of men, came to be more and more developed, especially under Domitian, and became a challenge to the Christians. The worship of the Emperor was

[1] *Provinces*, II, 199 n.

[2] W. M. Ramsay, *op. cit.* 246.

[3] This was the question in regard to which Pliny felt that he needed authoritative instruction.

disloyalty to Christ; it could not be regarded as a mere formality, but as a question touching the very foundations of society. There are traces of the Christian horror of this pretension in the *Second Epistle to the Thessalonians*[1], and in the *Apocalypse* (xiii. 4). Doubtless many Christians went as far as they conscientiously could in refraining from giving any excuse for the raising of the question; they were prepared to show their loyalty by swearing *per salutem Caesaris*, but not *per genium Caesaris*[2]; accusations of unworthy compliance roused mutual recrimination within the Church[3], and strengthened the suspicion of the authorities that the indisposition of the Christians to submit to military discipline was due to some inherent disloyalty on the part of the whole body.

The Roman Empire contained within itself the heritage of human civilisation as it had been developed in every part of the known world. It embraced the arts and the system of government that had grown up in the magnificent empires of the East, as well as the learning and political life of Greek Cities; the Empire had controlled the barbarous peoples of its extremities and brought them into its service. There was an enforcement of law and order throughout the whole area, and

---

[1] E. H. Askwith, *An Introduction to the Thessalonian Epistles*, 130 ff.

[2] W. M. Ramsay, *op. cit.* 323 n.

[3] Compare especially the attitude of the Montanists.

the great roads gave facilities for communication between its ports; they were planned for purposes of defence but they also served for commercial intercourse. The centre of the whole magnificent system was at Rome; all roads led to Rome, and the Emperor was the guiding power by whom the whole was maintained and ˏcontrolled. Local authorities and civic rights had lost their old independence and been absorbed in the great system of which the Emperor was the head. The religious question came to be of fundamental importance for the future of society. Should the irresponsible will of the Emperor be recognised as the ultimate authority in the affairs of men, or was it right to refuse him such homage, and to insist that Christ was a supreme ruler to whom even the Emperor was responsible? The Christians, while glad to show respect to the Empire and to take their part in maintaining the marvellous order which it had introduced and preserved throughout its provinces, were precluded from admitting of any human being that he was irresponsible, or of showing him the reverence that was due to God alone. This was the issue with which Christianity was confronted, especially in the times of Marcus Aurelius and Diocletian; and the triumph of the Cross was a victory over the pretensions of irresponsible tyranny. Even the most absolute rulers in Christendom have recognised their responsibility to God; and though the Prussian claim to wield resources of organised

culture without consideration for other peoples
has shown scant respect for Christianity either as a
doctrine of life or a guide to practice, it pays official
tributes to divine approval of its ambition.

36 The later Roman Empire was organised at
a new centre, and its extent was greatly
diminished by successive waves of barbarian invasion; but just because our own realm has been so
little in contact with it, we are apt to overlook its
importance as a polity. Mommsen[1] has expressed
the opinion that "Christianity was in reality not
"the enemy but the friend of the Empire," and that
"the Empire grew far stronger when its Emperors
"became Christian." Constantinople proved to be
a bulwark which stemmed the tide of Mohammedan invasion; we can best estimate the treasures
of art and learning it preserved, by noting the
extraordinary influence that was exercised in Italy
when the city fell at last in 1453 A.D., and when so
much of the heritage of ancient Rome was diffused
in the West. Amid the mutability of human affairs
Constantinople showed a marvellous stability;
it maintained an effective organisation and an
orderly life which present a striking contrast to the
chaos of the dark ages from which the lands that
had been torn from the Roman Empire slowly
emerged.

The Conversion of Constantine marks a great

[1] W. M. Ramsay, *op. cit.* 192, referring to Mommsen's
article in the *Hist. Zeitschrift*, XXVIII, 389 to 429.

change in the official position of the Emperor. He was still an autocrat; but he was so far from being absolute or unfettered in his caprices that he was regarded as the chief officer in a theocracy. There was no special religious significance in his coronation by the Patriarch[1]; but after the triumph over Arianism, no attempt was made to confer authority on a pagan or unorthodox Emperor, and his compliance was further secured by the terms of the coronation oath[2]. The change in the official attitude of the Emperor brought about a revolution in society for it immediately resulted in the Peace of the Church. The Christians, instead of being objects of suspicion[3] and liable to the punishment of death, were able to worship publicly and were in no danger from informers. They were no longer distracted by the care they had to exercise in taking their part in public duties without connivance in idolatrous rites. The Empire had ceased to be an embodiment of the evil in the world, and the Christians found themselves in a new environment. There was also a fundamental change in the whole character of the civilisation as it gradually worked out. The great code of Justinian treasured up and organised the tradition of Roman Law, and it served as a code for a Christian society. The building art was no longer directed to the erection of

[1] Bury, *Later Roman Empire*, 16.
[2] *Ibid*. 29.
[3] E. G. Hardy, *Studies in Roman History*, 38.

palaces and basilicas, it took a new development in the building of S. Sophia, and in the number of churches which were erected in Sicily[1] and in Sardinia as well as in Asia Minor. The new Platonism which had been cultivated at Alexandria, was eventually superseded by the Christian Philosophy of Clement and Origen; and the art of the orator was devoted to a new purpose by the great pulpit orators of the fourth century. The fabric of the later Roman Empire was entirely re-cast, and the glorification of the Emperor was no longer a main object; since all the resources of society were devoted to the glorification of Christ.

This remained a permanent difference between the East and the West. The Barbarians overran Italy and Gaul and Spain, as well as Africa; organised society was swept away and civilisation was reduced to fragments; Western Christendom had to be reconstructed, and built bit by bit from below upwards. But in the East no such destruction occurred; organised society remained, though it was transformed. The Christian revolution spread from above downwards, and from the centre outwards. The great crisis was in the imperial court itself; when that point was carried, the new religion which had penetrated into so many quarters was frankly adopted in the cities and among the educated classes. There was a long continued struggle in the rural districts, and an effort to retain and Christian-

[1] E. H. Freshfield, *Cellae Trichorae*, I, vii.

ise local festivals and local cults. But there were two types of institution which were planted as means of diffusing the Christian faith. S. Basil succeeded in building "an orphanage in every "district of his immense diocese. The one at "Caesarea with its church, bishops, palace and "residences for clergy, hospices for the poor, sick "and travellers, hospitals for lepers, and workshops "for teaching and practising trades was so large as "to be called the New City. Such establishments "constituted centres from which the irresistible "influence of the Church permeated the whole "district[1]." S. Basil also enlisted the services of monasticism to strengthen the Church. He brought "the monks into relation with the epis-"copate and established Coenobia in the towns "instead of the desert[2]," so as to be effective agents of the Catholic Church in place of the solitary hermits and anchorites who would have been a less powerful engine for affecting the country. The festivals with their local associations were not susceptible to the penetration of Christian influence; and the rural districts were the strongholds of paganism.

The decline and fall of the Roman Empire have been traced by a master hand, and subsequent investigations have tried to assign the causes, constitutional or economic, which were the main

[1] W. M. Ramsay, *op. cit.* 461.
[2] W. Lowther Clarke, *St Basil the Great,* 120.

reason of its decadence and loss of vitality. It may suffice to say that the later Empire was so organised as to give little scope for individual initiative. Bureaucracy had reduced political administration to a soulless routine, and there was little scope for enterprise in commercial life; the class of men who might have devoted themselves to the formation and employment of capital, were so far discouraged that the material resources of the Empire were not replenished and maintained; after Justinian there was little fresh inspiration as to the manner in which they might be employed.

37 The fall of Rome in 410 A.D. marks the complete disintegration of civilised society in the West; the desolation which the barbarians left behind them was complete; though the conquerors soon adopted the vices of the society they had swept away, they had no capacity for creating a social order where man might pursue his peaceful avocations without disturbance. Flourishing provinces were reduced to mere wilderness, and savage beasts re-asserted their dominance in places that had long been the homes of men[1]. The whole system of intercommunication and commerce had broken down; the cities could no longer depend on the supplies furnished by country districts or brought to them from abroad. The destruction was so complete that civilised society in the West had to be reconstructed from its very foundations.

[1] Montalembert, *The Monks of the West*, II, 316.

The adherents of paganism protested that the calamity was due to the spread of Christianity and the general forsaking of the worship of the old gods; and this complaint against the Christian religion was the occasion which S. Augustine used[1] to take up its defence. He had already pointed out that the Christian religion was quite compatible with all that was essential to a strong and vigorous polity[2]; and in the last ten books of the *City of God* he elaborated his argument and showed the ground of his hopes that a City of God would arise upon earth, which should control all temporal power and take the place of the Imperial City that had been destroyed. He had rejoiced in its greatness, in its civilisation, in its literature and philosophy; but he was not blind to the corruption which had infected it in every part and had rendered its destruction inevitable. He sketched a new order embodying new principles, which might take the place that the old had occupied, and he saw that the means were at hand by which these ideals might be realised. The aims which he delineated were consciously adopted for centuries in the efforts to reconstruct civilised society; and they still have an extraordinary hold in the present day on all who hold that it is the mission of the Church as an organised body to control the exercise of temporal power, whether they are Roman Catholics or Calvinists.

[1] *Retractationum Liber*, II, xliii, *Opera* (Migne), I. 647.

[2] *Epistolarum Classis III*, Ep. 138, *ad Marcellinum*, ii, *Opera* (Migne), II, 528.

One reason why his treatise on the *City of God* had such far reaching influence, is that S. Augustine endeavours to go to the very root of the matter in tracing the causes of the corruption and decay of the great Empire[1]. He traces them to the defect and perversity of the human will, and to the corruption and depravity which result. He thus devoted himself to enquiries which Ancient Philosophy had passed by, though the necessity of facing them has been felt in modern times[2]. As he analysed the cause of the corruption of society in self-will, he saw the possibility of an undying realm being introduced through the personal self-discipline for which the most effective conditions were given by Christian Monasticism.

The monastic ideal showed its wonderful effectiveness in the reconstruction of organised society in the West; but it had its limitations. It could provide for the disciplining of self-will and for the cultivation of detachment from sense; this is an Eastern ideal of the religious life and makes its constant appeal in Buddhism. Christian monastic life demanded a regular routine of work and study, but it was not a school for the cultivation of personal activity. Though it had an influence on civic and family life, it could not be the agent for transforming the whole of society. Family life and the providing for the future of the race lay outside its

---

[1] *Civitas Dei*, XII, vii, viii.

[2] Martineau, *Types of Ethical Theory*, I, 47.

scope, and it was not spiritual, in the sense of being able to pervade and transform all secular life, for it remained in some ways opposed to what was essential to secular life.

At the same time Latin Christianity could claim to be more deeply spiritual than the later Roman Empire. It could be urged that the Christianity of Byzantium was a mere veneer of a society that had been originally heathen, while Western Christendom was built up from below out of elements which were deeply impregnated with Christian habits of thought. The ultimate authority in the East lay with the Emperor, who might or might not be devout personally, but who as a civil officer exercised rule that was quite incompatible with the spiritual independence on which the Church in the West set such store. Monasticism was a factor in the christianisation of society in the East, but in the West it provided ideals which dominated Latin Christianity in all its aspects ; it initiated an entire reconstruction of society in Western Europe for which there was no need in the East.

II. SUPERSTRUCTURE IN THE WEST

38   Society in the West seemed to be completely disintegrated, but it was never reduced to such an aggregate of unrelated individuals as was imagined by seventeenth century theorists, who pictured the state of nature as a chaos from which civilisation had evolved. The feudal system, which

ultimately arose, was permeated throughout with the conception of contracts between individuals; but it did not have an original social contract as its basis. During some phases of the barbarian invasions there may have been a war of each against each, when the miserable refugees were reduced to the last extremities[1]; but such a state of war was not a long continued condition which called forth a conscious reaction and the establishment of a tyranny. The elements from which a new order was built up were the fragments of a great social system; not unrelated individuals, but individuals who retained some knowledge of the advantages of civilisation. They knew that co-operation might be favourable to their interests in the long run; and both in town and country there are traces of the survival of old institutions, or at any rate of the revival of similar institutions at such an early date that it seems probable that the ground had been prepared and the seeds sown under the ancient Empire. It is quite possible that the food supplies of Paris and of Bordeaux gave occasion for the maintenance of the organisation of those who brought corn to the market, at any rate the division of the city and the faubourgs at Le Mans and Dijon, suggest that there was no complete rupture of the historical continuity of these towns as inhabited places. Even though Uriconium and Silchester perished utterly, the occupation of the old sites at Exeter, London, York,

[1] Green, *Making of England*, 226.

and other places seems to show that the destruction
in Britain was not so complete as is sometimes
supposed; persistence in old methods of tillage,
and the existence of *villae* in the rural districts in
the times before the Norman Conquest, are most
easily accounted for on the supposition that Roman
rural life survived at a sufficient number of points
to hand on the tradition of cultivation as it had
existed in Roman Britain. The precise extent to
which Roman civilisation survived in the various
provinces of the Empire, and the manner in which
it was re-introduced, are problems which can only
be solved by careful investigations in each separate
locality; but it can hardly be a mere accident that
the area in Great Britain, which was surveyed in
Domesday Book under William the Conqueror, so
closely corresponded with the area over which the
organised institutions of the Roman Empire had
prevailed.

There was not a mere atomism in any of the
provinces of the Roman Empire, and reconstruction
did not arise by natural cohesion; there were
factors of authority and organising power which
brought the scattered elements gradually together.
The influence of episcopacy and monasticism can be
demonstrated by the importance which they had
in the new system, both as constructive and as
corrective, compared with the wholly subordinate
place which similar elements had occupied in the
old Empire. Christianity played an important part

in the reconstruction of Western Christendom, both in the authority which was exercised in monastic life, and in the organising power which was shown at many centres by the Bishops, especially by the Bishops of Rome.

There was one feature which was common to many parts of the Roman Empire, however different they might be in other respects. The territories had been laid out on a definite system by *agri mensores* and presented an appearance of regularity, which we can sometimes observe even now[1]; the land must have been somewhat like the chess-board country which Alice found when she passed through the looking glass. We can at least understand that the go-as-you-please methods of the German tribes must have seemed unsightly to the Roman eye[2]. Traces of centuriation are to be found in many parts of Britain, and they force us to feel that the civilisation of Rome had a very definite territorial character. When we hear of the organisation of the Church by the Roman missionaries to Britain, we are once more struck by the territorial character of the ecclesiastical system. The British and Columban churches were organised on a tribal basis; and the great controversy of the sixth and seventh centuries turned on the question whether ecclesiastical organisation should be framed on the territorial or tribal model. The tribal model sur-

[1] E.g. in the country near Brindisi.
[2] Tacitus, *Germania*, cap. xvi.

vived both in Ireland and in Wales; it was not till
after the Reformation that the parochial system
obtained a firm hold in Scotland. In England, on
the other hand, the territorial organisation of the
Church, which was exhibited by the building of
parish churches, had advanced very far before the
Norman Conquest; it was cemented and strengthened by the general recognition of the obligation
to pay tithes to the parish church. The growth
throughout the country of similar ecclesiastical
organisation on a territorial basis was an important
element in the growth of patriotism,—the recognition of a common country, as distinguished from
the consciousness of ties of blood. The progress of
constitutional freedom in England has been rendered
possible by the sense of a common country, and the
system of local representation; so long as the blood
tie, and tribal custom remains supreme[1], the
conditions are not present under which either local
government or local representation as we know
them can be effective.

39 While monasteries were important agencies
in the East for diffusing Christian civilisation
from above downwards, till it ousted or absorbed
the local cults, and the sacred places of paganism;
in the West monasteries were the chief instruments
for reconstructing a new social order from below.
They were Christian institutions, and owed their
existence to spiritual motives; they were organised

[1] W. J. Corbett, *Cambridge Mediaeval History*, II, 549.

with a view to the eradicating of self-will, and to the loyal acceptance of a Christian rule; but incidentally they had extraordinary effects upon society. It is generally recognised that the monks did much to preserve the remains of ancient learning through the dark ages; in the time of Aquinas the Christian tradition was strong enough to hold its own and to absorb Aristotelianism, as represented by Averrhoes, instead of being absorbed by it; but we do not always give the monks sufficient credit for preserving a knowledge of the arts of life. We can see how, from the time of the Roman mission onwards, the monks took pains over the management and improvement of their estates; and the monasteries were also centres at which the prosecution of industrial arts of many kinds were organised[1], and especially they proved to be schools of the building arts. Not only so, they had much to do with the beginnings of commercial life; their demand for supplies created a local market, and was besides the occasion for mercantile ventures and the beginnings of foreign commerce. It was under the shadow of and owing to the protection afforded by a great monastery that one after another of the towns of the Middle Ages sprang into life. As institutions they proved to be a most successful experiment in communism, and in the principle of rewarding men for their work according to their needs, and not according to the

[1] Cunningham, *Christianity and Economic Science*, 23.

worth of the product of their labour; and it is
impossible to say how much these principles, which
were recognised within the monastery, affected the
habits of those who established themselves in its
neighbourhood. They furnished concrete examples
of the working of the religious principles which
were in the air. The merchant gilds and the craft
gilds of the Middle Ages were for the most part
organised on a local basis, and with regard to civic
patriotism; but they had religious elements which
were common to all, and which showed themselves
not only in their alms and their association for
worship, but in the mutual helpfulness and regard
for the common interest which is seen in their
regulations.

40   The reign of Charles the Great was of
       supreme importance as it furnished the first
example of a type of Christian monarchy that fired
the imagination of other rulers for generations.
The Roman name had impressed mankind by the
glamour of its reputation, and gave extraordinary
support to the influence which was exercised on
the barbarian kings by the Roman pontiffs; but
Charles the Great set an example which our own
Alfred and other monarchs could imitate consciously. His coronation implied a recognition of
spiritual power in the conferring of civil authority,
such as was never admitted in the East. The long
period of reconstruction had so far advanced that
it was possible for Christianity not merely to defend

itself against the barbarians, but to take the
offensive for a time. The *Capitularies* tell of territorial administration which outlived tribal custom;
they mark too a step towards the recognition of
personal responsibility for crime[1],and, by enforcing
collective penalties, discouraged the sheltering of a
guilty person.

The services to the work of reconstruction, which
had been implicitly exercised by the influence and
organising power of the Papacy, came in the centuries which succeeded the death of Charles the
Great to be explicitly claimed; and the Emperors
were never able to command an effective power
such as was habitually exercised from Rome. Rome
proved itself to be the real ruler of Christendom
under the Papacy, as that city had formerly been
the centre of Imperial Authority; but yet there
were extraordinary differences. The roads were no
longer of importance as military highways to keep
the distant parts of Christendom in subjection;
itineraries show that they were mainly used for the
travels of civilians, either for pilgrimages, or for
commercial traffic. The popes were able to enforce
the adoption of a similar body of law throughout
the whole sphere of their influence; the Canon Law
contained much that was borrowed from the
Roman Law, and it dealt with many matters
which received little attention in the Barbarian
codes; the machinery for administering it and for

[1] B. S. Phillpotts, *Kindred and Clan*, 129.

the hearing of appeals on disputed points gave extraordinary influence to the Papacy throughout
Western Europe. The weakness of the Holy Roman
Empire was greatly due to the poverty of its
resources; but the Popes had a highly organised
fiscal system by means of which they were able to
rely on the regular receipt of an enormous revenue.
It was the work of Hildebrand to take the last steps
which were necessary to transform what had been
a spiritual influence, into an organised system, and
thus to render the Church more effective externally
in carrying on an open conflict; while its institutions
became less obviously the channels by which
divine power in the moulding of human wills and
human society made itself felt.

41　　Under Hildebrand the vision of S. Augustine
seemed to be most completely realised, and
there was one organised system in the known world
in which the spiritual power was supreme; earthly
ambitions and interests were relegated to a subordinate place; and yet how disappointing it
proved. It is from the time of Hildebrand that we
can note the increasing prevalence of the tendencies
which eventually brought about the disruption of
Christendom. The Church, as Hildebrand knew it
in his early days, was in danger of assimilating
itself to the conditions of ordinary life around;
there was a penetration of the secular spirit, and
ecclesiastical offices were treated as if they were
secular fiefs; while the clergy were in the habit of

providing for their children and dissipating the ecclesiastical heritage. Hildebrand set himself to detach the Church as an institution from the secular conditions which were proving so mischievous, and especially from the evil of simony; he was brought into conflict with civil power, in the person of the Emperor, and with the habitual adoption of family life which had become common among all the clergy who did not live by monastic rule in monastic institutions. He had extraordinary success in carrying out his policy. Henry IV was forced to make his peace at Canossa; the rule of celibacy was imposed upon the secular clergy and they were ruthlessly separated from their wives[1]. The Church became an institution detached from, and often antagonistic to the civil powers; and the clergy became a sacerdotal caste, which was freed from the ordinary obligation and duties of society, but was endowed with great possessions and capable of exercising enormous power in the world. This power had been most beneficent so long as it was an influence which guided and directed the secular powers, and of which they gladly availed themselves; but when the Church felt itself strong enough to exercise compulsion, and force men to adopt the ecclesiastical policy, it roused an immense amount of antagonism, and gave rise to institutions which apologists of the Church find it difficult to defend[2].

[1] H. Lea, *History of Sacerdotal Celibacy*, I, 236.
[2] Compare the judicial critique by Lord Acton of

The conflicts over investitures between the Pope and the Emperor, or between the ecclesiastical and civil power in a realm, did not make for the good of the community. There was need for the exercise of a high hand in putting down disorder and crime; even when ecclesiastical intervention did not foment disorder and occasion civil wars, the disparagement of civil authority and the organisation of ecclesiastical courts, which administered canon law in opposition to the law of the realm, introduced a state of affairs in which the public could look on the clergy as busily engaged in securing the privileges of their order rather than as devoting themselves to the good of the community.

The spread of heresy was a real evil which it was desirable to meet in order that Christian hopes and influences might continue to inspire improvement in society. Intellectualism has proved barren in Mohammedan lands, and never exercised the fruitful influence which came in the fifteenth century from humanism; but the parable of the Tares had given a warning for all time against the mistake of trying to extirpate heresy by such institutions as the Inquisition, or by instigating the civil authorities to punish it as a crime. We cannot specify any definite date when these attempts began, and excuses for compulsion and persecution can be

Mr Lea's *History of the Inquisition* in *The English Historical Review* (Oct. 1888), III, 773.

found in S. Augustine[1] and have apparent claims
to scriptural authority[2]; but from the time of
Hildebrand onwards when the detachment of the
Church from secular life became more complete,
there was an increased tendency to rely on strength-
ening the hold of Christianity by compulsion and
force, instead of relying on spiritual influence and
censures for working insensibly in the right direction.

42 In the effort to diffuse Christianity in the
world Christendom put forth its full strength,
and it was by the Crusades that the method of
compulsion was completely discredited. The military organisation of the Roman Empire had broken
down; it had failed to defend itself against the
incursions of barbarians and one after another of
the provinces had been torn from it. But Christendom had at length become strong enough by the
method of peaceful penetration to aim, not merely
at self-defence, but at enlarging its borders.
Charles the Great's campaigns against the Saxons
were organised in accordance with the political aim
of securing his positions from attack, but missionary
zeal was apparently combined with the political
aim in these expeditions; they certainly gave the
opportunity for the planting of new centres of
Christian influence, and the nominal acceptance
of Christian principles disarmed much of the old

---

[1] *Epist.* XLIII *ad Vicentium*, c. v.
[2] Bp. Creighton, *Persecution and Tolerance*, 60.

hostility. There was a great extension of the area of Christendom when the Kings of Hungary accepted the faith; and though Heathenism held its own in the Baltic lands for long, the vigour of Christendom was mainly directed against the barrier which Mohammedanism had erected, since it prevented the passage of pilgrims to the lands that had been the scene of the earthly life of Christ.

Till the evils of feudalism were repressed by the rise of strong central monarchies, the horrors of ruthless war and of private war were constantly breaking out, and quarrels tended to perpetuate themselves; a perverted sense of duty would not let bygones be bygones, but insisted on attempting to exact vengeance. The Church seems to have exercised an extraordinary influence in northern France by obtaining respect for the peace of God, and for the truce of God[1], so that there was a close time when fighting might not take place, and when the industrial population might secure a measure of protection from the ravages of war. There came to be a new standard for the conduct of soldiers; the tradition of chivalry, which still distinguishes between the clean fighter and the inhuman practices of the mere brute, is a legacy which has come down to us from the knightly orders of the Middle Ages.

There was too a great gain in consecrating the militarism of the Middle Ages, so that skill and courage should no longer be used for selfish and

[1] Semichon, *La paix et la trêve de Dieu*, I, 36.

personal objects, but should be consecrated by
being devoted to the highest purposes. All manly
gifts and physical powers may be subordinated
and directed to the public good and to a divine
purpose, they come to take a new character when
they are consciously pursued with such high aims.
But in retrospect we see that the high level could
not be maintained, and that the reliance on military
force and the arm of the flesh has degraded the
ends in view. The habitual reliance on the exercise
of Temporal Power was hardly compatible with
single hearted devotion to spiritual influence. The
religious object, which inspired the preaching of
Peter the Hermit and the masses which followed
him, could only be attained by wresting territory
from Moslem hands, and organising the Holy Land
as a piece of Christendom. The attainment of
victory, the control of territory, and the establishment of a Latin Kingdom at Jerusalem came to be
the immediate objects of the crusaders; and every
sort of mercantile interest was willing to co-operate
with them in their undertaking. The whole movement was the occasion for an immense amount of
intrigue and opportunism, which consorted badly
with the great spiritual enthusiasm with which the
first efforts had been undertaken. Failure to maintain the initial successes reacted most unfavourably
on the reputation of Christendom as an organised
society, while the prominence given to militarism,
and the contact with Eastern thought and manners,

introduced many undesirable elements into Western
Christendom. The Crusades and their final failure
did much to show how completely the Papacy had
come to resemble secular powers in relying on
physical force and intrigue, and how much it had
ceased to exercise an influence that was really
spiritual.

III. THE DISRUPTION OF CHRISTENDOM

43   The more we examine it, the more may we
feel how far reaching and deep was the
change which was wrought in Western Europe by
the Reformation, and the less we shall be satisfied
to try and find one formula which applies to it in
all its aspects. It was not merely a negative movement which devoted itself to the criticism of abuses
in the Church of the day. The organised institutions of the fifteenth century were necessarily
different from the arrangements which served for
the scattered congregations of apostolic times, and
the literalists, who took the records of the past as
giving a model for all ages of time, found much to
condemn by their standard. The clergy had come
to be an unpopular caste; they had ceased to be
the leaders of economic or constitutional improvement, or to undertake the rôle which they had
discharged in the dark ages, and they were blamed
far and wide; but it was not by merely returning
to the simplicity of a bygone age that an advance
could be made. The reforms, which would have

satisfied Savonarola and other spiritually-minded
men or Erasmus and other lovers of learning could
have been incorporated in the existing system;
they might have delayed, but they would hardly
have prevented the revolution. The positive principle which lay behind many aspects of the time,
was an insistence on the importance of secular life[1];
this brought all the scattered elements of discontent
to a focus, and is the distinguishing feature of
modern as contrasted with mediaeval times. Even
the counter-revolution of the Jesuits showed an
appreciation of secular life and a recognition of
the claims of new learning and new aspirations, which were a great departure from the
attitude of the mediaevalists, who had found an
ideal in detachment from secular life altogether.
Luther's dramatic opposition to the established
powers gave him a personal prominence, which no
reformer before his time had attained and which
marked him out from all his contemporaries;
though a reliance on individual conviction braced
him to play his own part, the principle for which he
contended may be most conveniently summarised
as that of the importance in the sight of God of
secular life. For him Christianity did not consist
only in detachment from the secular and the
attractions of sense, it had a power to use secular
activities and powers for the highest ends, and to

[1] F. D. Maurice, *Kingdom of Christ*, I, 72; *Life*, I, 320,
325.

bring every thought of the mind into obedience to Christ. His own experience had rendered him dissatisfied with the monastic life which had once kindled his enthusiasm; he had found protection from the forces which were prepared to crush his convictions in the action of a secular prince. Conscious responsibility to God for the use made of human powers was an inner principle which could consecrate all human activities; by dominating the inner life it could render religion not only compatible with progress but a motive and guide to pursue it. There was a close correspondence, which Luther partly perceived, between the work of S. Paul, in trusting to inner principle and discarding the external ordinances of Judaism, and his own work, in protesting against the restraint that had been imposed in the supposed interest of organised spiritual life, and in insisting on faith,— that is the sense of personal responsibility to God,— as the controlling power which might mould self-will, and render life religious.

44   The Renaissance had done much to prepare for the assertion of this positive principle, and to prepare men to accept it. Admiration had been directed to the glories of ancient civilisation, and the virtues which had been cultivated in pagan times. Humanism was a protest against the sordid character of life in the later Middle Ages; against monkish contentment with ignorance, and the opportunism and ambition of political factions. The

contrast with paganism at its best had been striking, and gave effective grounds for criticising existing society. But Humanism had no regenerative power; it was a mere revival which took its inspiration from a dead past, and the efforts it aroused after imitation degenerated into pedantry. Europe could only be saved by accepting new ideals, and not by attention to the niceties of grammar. Humanism was an important element; but in Italy it was largely a reaction against Christendom as it had existed in the fifteenth century, and was ready to set itself in opposition to the good as well as to the evil in the existing system. The strength of Western Christendom, and its success in reconstructing society after the barbarian invasions, had been due to the means it afforded for the discipline of the human will. The excesses and scandals which accompanied the Renaissance seem to show that it could suggest no effective bridle for self-will, but was ready to find excuses for a self-indulgent life, and to glorify passion. The tendency to call evil good affected both private and public life, and Machiavelli's treatment of the art of government as non-moral seemed to justify the most unscrupulous action on the part of the Prince.

45   There was a new element in the awakening to fuller consciousness of belonging to a common country. There is abundant evidence that in England, at all events, the civic patriotism and local attachments of an earlier period were

being superseded by this larger patriotism. There is abundant evidence of the growth of this feeling for a common country in the *Libell of English Policye*, and the *Debate of the Heralds*; in the acceptance of the Tudor despotism which stamped out the discordant elements, and in the national sentiment which became dominant in the spacious days of Queen Elizabeth. The Crown and the Council had the means of controlling local administration throughout the realm, and of creating a solidarity which made it possible to enforce a common policy in regard to social and economic questions within the realm, as well as in international relations. The towns and their gilds were no longer able to pursue an independent policy, without regard to the welfare of the realm as a whole; and the duty of every part to co-operate for the common good was insisted upon in numberless statutes and by the action of the Council. There had been complaint from time immemorial that the Church with its vast estates did not bear its fair share of the burdens which were needed for the government of the realm. Edward II attacked the Templars, on whose military powers the defence of the realm was not a first charge; there was much grumbling about the alien priories, and about the vast amounts of money which went out of the country for the use of a foreign potentate. The grievances of generations came to a head in Tudor times; this was a period of rapid agricultural progress

when convertible husbandry and several cultivation were coming into vogue instead of the old
common fields; the impoverishment, from which
the monasteries suffered, may be compared with
their prosperity in previous days and makes it
improbable that they were able to move with the
times, and probably the government was justified
in thinking that a large area of land was not being
put to the most profitable use in the public interest.
That under these circumstances the land should be
confiscated was quite in accordance with the spirit
of the times, which would have supported the royal
right to resume into its own hands property that did
not co-operate for the public interest; but there is
no reason to suppose that either Thomas Cromwell
or the ministers of Edward VI were scrupulous in
the pretexts they put forward to give an apparent
justification to their actions. Ample evidence
exists to show that the dissolution of the monasteries
was a shock to the religious feeling of many parts
of the country[1]; but if the country was to have
any real cohesion it was necessary that the outposts
of a foreign power should be swept away.

England attained to a solidarity that was much
more complete than that of other realms; but still
the claims of the monarchies showed that important
steps had been taken towards the unifying of
Scotland, of France and of Spain into nations

[1] F. Rose-Troup, *The Western Rebellion of 1549*, 126;
compare also the Pilgrimage of Grace.

which were conscious of a common country. Ecclesiastical jealousy had co-operated with commercial rivalry to give force to the Scottish demand for independence from England, and the Christian religion served as a bond of union which united the peoples of Castile and Arragon in their struggle with the Moors of Grenada. But there was no real blending of different classes in a common national life in Spain; clan feeling survived in many parts of Scotland; and even in France, where the monarchy was very strong and wonderfully well served, the organs of local governments were sufficiently powerful to prevent the enforcing of a common internal policy till the time of the Revolution. In England the Stuarts were able to make use of the local institutions as agents for promoting national improvements; and other countries had a growing consciousness of unity which showed itself in efforts after national improvement as well as in the struggles of international rivalry.

46 The desire to pursue a national policy, to promote national improvement, and the readiness to engage in international rivalry brought the rulers and the people of various European countries into direct antagonism with the efforts of the Roman court to maintain a cosmopolitan policy. The time had passed when the energies of all parts of Christendom could be directed into a common assault on Saracen power; it was in Portugal[1], where the crusading enthusiasm had

---

[1] Beazley, *Prince Henry the Navigator*, 78, 124.

survived, that there were systematic efforts to explore and to circumvent the barriers by which the Moslem people were confining Christendom. The age of discovery opened up possibilities of access to all parts of the world, and all the trading people were ready to insist on their right to have a share in the scramble which had begun for the command of these new resources. Alexander VI, by attempting to decide between the respective claims of Spain and Portugal, made a fatal mistake in ignoring the possibilities of progress in northern lands. Cosmopolitanism was ready to secure a peace by which the realms of greatest strength should be helped to maintain their existing superiority, and the future of the smaller nations should be sacrificed. The papal tradition then as now was in favour of such a peace as would enable the realm that was strongest at the moment to exploit the other peoples of mankind; but the rising nationalities were unwilling to part with their birthright in the sixteenth century. The seafaring peoples of the north took up the challenge of the papacy and demanded its authority to intervene and make such a division of the terrestrial globe. By what authority doest thou these things? The sea power of England at the discovery of the New World, and later of Holland and of France, refused to abide by this decision; and though the precise lines of cleavage were not drawn till the seventeenth century, open revolt from the papal pretension had begun, and there was a disruption of Christendom, which shows little prospect of being healed.

47 The open defiance of papal authority in regard to political affairs rallied round it the various elements of discontent and disapproval, and consolidated the consciousness of national life which has been the great feature of modern times; this has become more and more prominent in the nineteenth century with the union of Italy, the consolidation of Germany under one Ruler, and the closer sense of common life which has arisen throughout the United States and expresses itself in enthusiasm for the one flag. But at the first, the progress of the Reformation seemed to be merely destructive of the basis on which cosmopolitan peace and social morality had rested. The religious wars of the sixteenth century crushed the prosperity of Flemish and Italian towns, and devastated France, while the Thirty Years' War threw German development back for a couple of centuries. The defiance of papal authority in public life gave occasion for refusing to respect its pronouncements in regard to business morality or private life, and afforded the disreputable elements of society an opportunity to assert themselves. Though the fruits of the Reformation seemed so disastrous, it was possible to maintain that the roots of the evil lay very deep, and that the Church of Rome, in attempting to rule and control all political and secular life, had exceeded her commission and lost her spiritual character.

National authorities came to insist that they had themselves a duty in regard to the religious life of the people committed to their charge by God, and that they were not justified in standing aside and acquiescing in the inability of the cosmopolitan authority to check ecclesiastical abuses and scandals. The duty of national authority to intervene was strongly felt by the Spanish Monarchs, and resulted in the re-organisation of ecclesiastical institutions and the development of the Holy Office, wherever Spanish power was felt; it was shown in the assertion of Gallican liberties in France, and in Germany by the action of Charles V in the Interim[1], and in pressing for the summoning of the Council of Trent. But it was most drastically carried through by Henry VIII and Elizabeth, who broke the cosmopolitan connection altogether, and encouraged the maintenance of ecclesiastical institutions, with diminished wealth and influence, but on national lines.

The defiance of papal authority by some national powers, and the relative disregard of it by others, led to an increase of absolutism on the part of civil authorities; attempts were made to justify this absolutism by insistence on the powers of the monarchy as inherent and personal. The mediaeval doctrine had regarded the prince as holding his power as a trust to be exercised for the welfare of his people; but those who contended that the pope

[1] *Cambridge Modern History*, II, 264.

had no authority to judge as to the monarch's faithfulness to his trust, tended to insist that the monarch's power was inherent or was directly given by God; so that the King exercised his civil authority by a divine right, and with no responsibility to the judgment of a foreign potentate or to that of his own subjects. The Jesuits gave precision to the claims of the papacy to have authority to release subjects from allegiance to monarchs who were judged unfaithful to their trusts; an alliance was thus effected between the claims of the papacy to supreme authority over earthly monarchs on the one hand, and democratic political principles on the other.

The sixteenth and seventeenth centuries concerned themselves much with discussions as to the basis of political authority and the forms of government; there were many advantages in the organisation of all the institutions of a country under one head; the inability of Holland, where a federal system was adopted, to pursue a common policy persistently, eventually led to her downfall. Monarchical government approved itself as the best form for practical purposes; but as Aristotle had pointed out, there might be a good and a bad government under very similar forms, and a monarchy might easily degenerate into a tyranny. The security against bad government really lies not in any form of government, nor in any system of checks on government, but in an inner principle—

a sense of responsibility and duty on the part of the ruler. The evil of tyranny lies not in the existence of power, but in the misuse of power; it was only by a constant care to use his power as a trust for which he was responsible to God, and with a regard not merely for his own interests but for the welfare of his people, that a Christian prince could discipline himself for the exercise of his office aright.

The common weal also supplied a secular object for the sake of which a man might rightly be called to discipline himself; the Elizabethan times in England were an era when enthusiasm for the realm of England and devotion to the person of the monarch were curiously blended; but no community can be at its best unless the individual is willing habitually to sacrifice his private interests, and even if need be his life, for the common weal. The changes from personal monarchy to democracy have been changes in the mode in which the call to sacrifice has come; and it is very rarely that the call to make the supreme sacrifice has come as loudly and as generally as it has done at the present time; but the spirit of individual sacrifice of private convenience and of personal possession must be present, or the organisation of society cannot be maintained: that public spirit can be counted upon is the first condition for the existence of a civil society that is both well ordered and free.

The monastic life in mediaeval Christendom had offered opportunities for self-discipline, with a view to participating in the life to come; the life of a democratic citizen offers opportunities for disciplining himself for doing his duty in the life that now is. Monastic life cultivated detachment from things of sense as a cure for self-indulgence ; the life of citizenship calls for the exercise of all the activities and energies of life for the common good. This is in accordance with the Reformation ideals, for it lays stress on the worth of secular life, and on the discharge of responsibilities by activity in the exercise of powers and privileges, and not merely on self-repression. It recognises the need of spiritual power, not merely as an external system which works from without, but as an influence which gives new force, and maintains the purity of the inner life.

48   It is the condition of progress in modern life that we should be constant in aiming at the common weal, and ready to learn by experience as to the habits we must cultivate and the means we can employ to realise it more and more completely. We may be ready, too, to rely on the experience which is gathered from day to day, both as to the cultivation of the spiritual life within, and as to the best means of ordering social life. There have, however, been powerful tendencies at work, among those peoples who broke away from Latin Christendom, to set up some new standard as absolute, in place of the cosmopolitan authority which had been defied.

Calvinism insisted as strongly as the papacy had done on the existence of spiritual authority to lay down rules for social and political life; but it declared that the papacy had long ceased to be the true Church, and that the Bible furnished a standard to be applied to all the relations of life. Calvin believed that he found in the accounts of the apostolic age explicit directions for Church organisation from which the Roman Church had gradually and completely departed; but he held that as soon as the Church was reformed in accordance with divine directions, it should exercise control over civil powers. He carried out his system by establishing ecclesiastical authority in Geneva; and John Knox was successful in displacing the "synagogue of Satan," and in preparing the way for the establishment of ecclesiastical discipline as the supreme authority in the Scottish nation. Indeed the organisation of ecclesiastical institutions in parish schools and churches was carried out so effectively on a territorial basis in Scotland, that Calvinism contributed not a little to the superseding of tribal and local divisions there by diffusing a sense of possession of a common country.

But though the Bible, as a record of personal religious experience, is of the highest value for the cultivation of the personal religious life, it is a mistake to treat it as giving a code which can be authoritatively enforced in political or social life. The pretension of the ministers to the authority of the Old Testament prophets and to exercise political control was terribly mischievous in Scotland, and was never able to assert itself in England. The lack of historical sense in treating the institutions of Israel as binding on Christian people for all time led to a revival of a religious society, which had many analogies with the Jewish theocracy, but which had no power to discriminate and oppose the abuses which came to light with the progress of Capitalism. When Dr Chalmers announced that the laws of Political Economy were a divinely instituted counterpoise to the laws of Nature[1], there was no wonder that the working classes should be encouraged to assert that ecclesiasticism of every kind was prepared to give its sanction to the oppression of the poor at the hands of the rich.

On the other hand, the mischievous influence of Anabaptist principles was obvious even in the sixteenth century; they were intensely repugnant to Luther, who saw in them a caricature of his own teaching, and there is frequent allusion to their errors in the Thirty-nine Articles. The Anabaptists used their spiritual principles to strike at the existence of well ordered society; they denied that a Christian citizen was justified in exercising the powers which are essential to public life. Since the Bible gave a sufficient guide for duty as private individuals, they were unwilling to admit exceptions to these rules for private conduct, in

[1] *Christian and Civic Economy of Large Towns*, III, 36, 37.

the interest of the State. They did not respect the office of a magistrate, since it required him to punish crime instead of forgiving injuries; the citizen who desired to act as a Christian was bound to refuse to give evidence on oath, or to support his prince in the defence of the realm by taking up arms. Moreover, while Calvinism and the pretensions to enforce a biblical code have lost their political importance, the Anabaptist habit of mind has been perpetuated and has spread; there is a large body of opinion in favour of the neglect of public responsibilities of every kind, and an indisposition to acknowledge the duty of obedience to civil authority, which is incompatible with the existence, and still more with the progress of well ordered society.

Private interests of every sort and disregard of the duties of citizenship have taken shelter under the religious principles of the Anabaptists; men will only support the community so far as their own interest dictates; they resent any claim for sacrifice. But the welfare of the future cannot be secured without sacrifice in the present, and the welfare of the community demands the sacrifice of private interests from time to time. The community is free and strong in which such sacrifices are made willingly and by consent, and not merely enforced by central authority.

The principle that attention to private duty will suffice to bring about improvements in society, and that there is no need for the community to enforce favourable conditions, has not commended itself in experience. George Fox had denounced the evil of slavery; but Woolman met with comparatively little success a century later, in rousing his co-religionists to a sense of its heinousness. It was only when it became the subject of public discussion in civil assemblies that its hold upon society was threatened. William Penn hoped that a personal understanding with Indians, who had been disarmed, might have as much force as a public treaty in securing immunity from attacks, but he found before long that it was necessary for the community to organise a system of common defence. The private efforts of individuals have often done much by the way of experiment to show the possibility of improvement, but the arm of the law has been necessary to render the improvement general, or to maintain it as permanent in society.

X

UNITED WITNESS TO CHRIST

I. DIFFERENT DENOMINATIONS

49 Since the fifteenth century Christendom has ceased to give a united witness for Christ to the world. There was of course much friction in the mediaeval world—the rivalry of seculars with regulars and between different Orders, and the disputes of various schools of thought; but we should not overlook the fact that after all the organised system bore constant witness to two great truths. It testified against the right of any rulers, however great, to exercise arbitrary power, and insisted on the responsibility of princes to God; and it maintained that the personal life of Man was not to be gauged or guided merely with reference to material things, but that it was his bounden duty to view this life as a part of his undying life. In the Middle Ages there was a constant and habitual witness to spiritual truths of which we in modern times are apt to lose sight.

The attempt to maintain a national witness to Christ was strongly in the minds of the reformers of the sixteenth century. It was the motive at work, when the parliament of Scotland endorsed the confession of Christian faith which had commended itself to the Assembly of the Church in that land[1]; it was an element which inspired Drake with an eagerness to plant in the new world the Christian faith, as the English Church and realm had received the same, and to protest against the subjection of distant races to the Spanish system[2]. But during the seventeenth century the effort to devise a national system which should perpetuate the Christian faith within the realm, and witness to the world without, proved impracticable. The disruption of Christendom had been the precursor of many movements by which the Christian Church was broken into the merest fragments; and though individuals, by their saintly lives, continued to give a personal witness for Christ, there were many who abandoned the very conception of national witness and of corporate witness altogether[3].

The close of the nineteenth century brought about a reaction in many protestant countries, and a sense that a visible unity among Christians, and a united witness to Christ are necessary conditions for greater success in missionary work among the heathen abroad, and for rousing from indifference to religion at home. There is a constant demand that professing Christians should sink their differences; and ecclesiastical leaders are more

---

[1] Cunningham, *Christianity and Politics*, 65.

[2] Fletcher *The World Encompassed by Sir Francis Drake*, 124, 132.

[3] Cunningham, *Christianity and Politics*, 92.

ready than they have been since the time of the
English Revolution to consider or devise schemes
for comprehension.

The precise reasons for the non-success of the
schemes for international religious union between
Anglicanism and Lutheranism, or for the failure of
Bishop Ussher's and Bishop Burnet's schemes for
the comprehension of presbyterians and episco-
palians in Great Britain and Ireland, are a matter of
history; and it is unnecessary to rake up the embers
of forgotten controversies; but it may be doubted
whether the method of compromise and comprehension is really sound, or is ever likely to prove an
effective means of accomplishing the end in view,
and restoring a united witness to Christ. We may
compromise about the externals of ecclesiastical
organisation, or about the externals of worship,
and consent to try to adapt ourselves to the habits
of other people; but religious conviction is a matter
of the inner life about which there can be no compromise; we cannot vary the beliefs that inspire
our conduct at pleasure or out of mere politeness.
Willingness to do so would tend to defeat its own
object; there can be no united witness to truth,
unless we are each prepared to hold fast to that
which we trust, and to Him in whom we have
believed. We cannot regard any religious opinions
which we are ready to compromise, as being a
sacred trust which it is our duty to hand on to
future generations and to plant in distant places.

The method of comprehension is also unsatisfactory, as a means of healing the divisions of Christendom and securing a united witness, since it only attempts to draw the line of division at new points—to include what is at present excluded at the risk of excluding what is at present included. It is useless to look at the circumference and decide where we shall draw the line; the organised Free Churches in this country are inclined to hold aloof from Unitarians, even though they profess and call themselves Christians. The practical Christianity of many Agnostics and the good citizenship of many Jews are generally recognised. It is not for any of us to decide at what point we shall draw a line, but to be loyal in maintaining spiritual truth which shall serve as a rallying point to men of different temperaments and upbringing. Spiritual power is able to mould the individual will, and to set old formulas in a new light; in so far as it works from within outwards, it will produce an organic unity which involves no dishonest compromise but is a witness to united conviction.

50   The reality of spiritual power, as something that breaks the bonds of habit and changes character, has been exhibited again and again in the lives of particular men who have put their personal experience on record; the accounts of the struggles of S. Augustine and of John Bunyan are widely known; there have been thousands in all ages who have felt themselves face to face with

eternal realities, and have been conscious of sin and remorse; and conscious too of divine forgiveness, as a call to enter on a new life. The earnestness of their endeavours to make their convictions the rule of their lives has impressed itself on their neighbours, and the accumulated effect has modified the tone of society and altered its habits. "Life "develops from within"; the changes by which the slavery and vices of pagan Rome have been superseded by the wide diffusion of higher ideals of life and the fitful effort to realise them, has not been initiated by compulsion from without, but by the personal earnestness and example of individual men, who have felt the power of the world to come and have yielded themselves to its influence.

Spiritual power is not confined in its exercise by any material conditions, but it may make any incident or any circumstances the occasion of its operation. Whatever may be its usual mode of action, and whatever readiness there may be to yield to it, there are, so far as we can observe, no conditions of place and time to which it is necessarily confined; this was the truth which was manifested to S. Peter, on his visit to Cornelius. There is the greatest variety of operations, and we shall do well to recognise the work of God's Spirit, wherever there is a real sense of duty, and an effort to be guided by unselfish aims, and not by passion or personal advantage. God's Spirit is not restricted to any one mode of operation. It is important that we should be ready to recognise change of character, and unselfishness of purpose as evidence of the work of God's Spirit; and should welcome it by whatever channel it may have operated. The peoples of northern Europe have shaken themselves free from the belief that certain external organisation was the necessary condition of the bestowal of God's Grace, and they are not prepared to regard any particular series of inner experiences as essential to that consciousness of personal communion with God which the psalmist valued above all earthly things. Nor need we attempt to apply any absolute standard in regard to the good and bad of men's opinions; we may be content with that which our Lord has laid down so far as we can apply it. "By their fruits ye shall know them,"—by their efforts to realise God's will in the world, so far as they see it. We are so apt to apply some standard of consistency which appeals to our own minds. We have not the knowledge to approve or condemn as divine wisdom can do, and to judge of others individually by the use they make of their opportunities. It is enough for each of us to be earnest in trying to make the most of our own, whatever they may be.

This sense of the exactingness of the divine judgment should rouse to an eagerness in pursuing the strenuous life and in doing the duties that come to hand; and also to the effort to make the most of our own lives, and cultivate our own powers of knowing and feeling. The philosopher seeks to make the best thought of all the ages his own, and the artist to appreciate the beauty in which the noblest feeling of each age has found expression; and the religious man should not be content to neglect the heritage of spiritual experience which he has received in the traditions of the past. He may seek to enter personally into the religious experience of the holy men of old who served God in their day and generation, and even to share the thoughts and aspirations of that Son of Man who felt Himself to be the Son of God.

51   Eagerness to cultivate the inner life personally involves a willingness to accept encouragement which comes from any quarter. We have no right to stigmatise any human being as one in whom God's Spirit cannot work, and from whom we may not ourselves learn. It was the error of the Pharisees that they felt they had nothing to learn from the people who knew not the Law; and it is this superciliousness which prevents so many from knowing the day of visitation. Christians are called upon not only to make the most of their own lives, but to perpetuate the knowledge of God as Christ has manifested it, so that it may be an inspiration in all coming generations. The full realisation of the intimate relations of God and Man was manifested to the world in the life and words of our Lord; and this has been confirmed by multitudes who have been conscious that He is the

guide to whom they may trust for insight and strength to lead their lives manfully. There is a duty to keep this knowledge of God alive in the world, lest men should be content with the less complete knowledge of God and of themselves which prevailed before Christ came, and should fall back into the lethargy and hopelessness which it engendered.

While we may each be willing to learn from every quarter for ourselves, we may also feel that experience can help us to see how best the knowledge of the power of Christ may be kept alive and transmitted among men. Our Lord gave it as a trust to His Apostles that it should be so transmitted; He has instituted rites which speak in every land and age of His personal care for each and all, and set forth the redeeming power of His undying Love. We may feel that even if these sacraments are not to be regarded as exclusive means which limit the possibility of the working of the Spirit to particular manifestations, they are the means which Christ enjoined us to use for perpetuating the knowledge of Him to the generations to come; and we have no right to deem ourselves wiser than He was, and to disregard or think lightly of His command.

Christians may err if, in their eagerness to commend Him as Master to the present generation and in the circumstances of the present stage of culture, they lightly condemn any age of the past as utterly unworthy and godless; or deny that Christ has fulfilled His promise to abide continually with His people. Christendom did preserve the knowledge of Christ, and there was no need to start anew and denounce the synagogue of Satan. The sacred writings which the Calvinists took as the code for political and personal life in their new theocracy had been treasured and preserved in the monasteries which were swept away. There has been frequent change in the circumstances and opportunities of human life, and there has been a constant need of adaptation in order to bring the knowledge of Christ to bear as a living power in the new order; but though different ecclesiastical forms and institutions have arisen and the old have been superseded, it is unwise to pronounce an absolute condemnation, or to fancy that we must start afresh. The truths which come home to one generation do not cease to be true because they are less applicable and fall into the background under other circumstances; no one age is equally alive to all aspects of Christian truth; still less is it possible for any one person to attain such complete Christian experience that there is no room for better apprehension of the Love of God. Each Christian can witness most effectively to what has come within his personal experience, but he must feel his own limitations in the eyes of God. "Regard not our "sins but the faith of Thy Church," is the prayer of each generation in turn. The truth of God is a larger thing than the power of apprehension in any age, still more than the power of apprehension in any individual mind[1]. The Vincentian maxim does not serve as a test for accurate expression for all time; it reminds us that the re-assertion of truths, which seem to have lost their application to our circumstances, may be needed in time to come. Consciousness of actual connection with the distant past when our Lord led His earthly life, and of responsibility for executing the trust He imposed, is to be cherished as a help to those who seek to keep the knowledge of Him alive for ages yet to come. A recognition of spiritual consciousness as the manifestation of the Power which has been working in the world and has never been wholly withdrawn is the best antidote to the narrowness of our own lives and our readiness to condemn others.

II.   CAUSES OF DIFFERENCE

52   Spiritual influences operate on human life in all of its aspects, political and intellectual,

---

[1] Edward Irving used very severe language of Evangelicalism, "which denies any gift of God either in the work of "Christ or in the sacraments, or anywhere until we experi- "ence it to be within ourselves, making God a mere "promiser, until we become receivers; making his bounty "and beneficence nought but words, till we make it reality "by accepting thereof; in one word making religion only "subjective in the believer, and not elective in God,— "objective in Christ, in order that it may be subjective "in the believer; a religion of moods and not of purposes "and facts; having its reality in the creature, its proposal "of reality only in God." *Confessions of Faith*, p. xcix.

as well as ecclesiastical; differences on purely secular matters, such as the basis of civil authority, have an affinity with one or another belief in regard to spiritual life and react so as to bring about religious differences in the community.

This is most easily seen in the history of England and Scotland during the seventeenth century. The age had inherited the conception of a Christian Community from the Middle Ages, and was eager to create a Christian Society which should be in accordance with the mind of Christ in all its principles and methods of administration. John Wesley made a new departure, since he realised, as his immediate predecessors failed to do, the importance of bringing the gospel message home to individuals personally; and in pursuing this aim he felt justified in disregarding the ecclesiastical and territorial organisation on which he himself had laid such stress in his work in Georgia; but till his time it was the creation of a Christian Common Weal[1] which was the aim of the leaders of all religious parties, of John Knox and Andrew Melville in Scotland and Laud in England, as well as of the Pilgrim Fathers; despairing of the corruption in the old world, they sought to plant theocracies in the new world. The principles which moved men at that time were principles as to the organisation of Christian Society, rather than as to the devout life of individuals. The Friends were

[1] E. Troeltsch, *Soziallehre*, 448.

ostracised by all other sects; and we can only understand the bitterness against them when we remember that they had no doctrine of Christian Society, but seemed to be mere religious anarchists, who laid stress on private conduct and refused to take their part in the duties of citizenship. The Scots relied on what they believed to be scripture principles in their efforts to organise a theocracy, and insisted on maintaining the office of a king as head of the community, while the history of the English inclined them to experiment in other forms of government. But the various religious sects which sprang into life in the seventeenth century were primarily actuated by principles for the organisation of civil society in regard to which divine authority is, not now claimed. Divisions remain, though the principles, for which men formerly sacrificed their lives, rarely find expression at all[1]; they are for the most part forgotten even by those parties which owe to them their separate organisation; they would be repudiated by the descendants of men who regarded them as matters of vital importance.

It is unnecessary to go back on these political causes of division in detail, as the crisis through

---

[1] The declaration of the Free Presbytery of Inveraray that the conscription of ministers by the State was inconsistent with the principle of Spiritual Independence of the Church as recognised in the Treaty of Union is so exceptional as to be a mere curiosity. *Northern Chronicle*, 25 April, 1917.

which the nation is passing has given an illustration of the manner in which differences in regard to political duties may cause fresh cleavage in ecclesiastical organisations. Those who regard the dictates of the individual conscience as supreme for each man, and regard the claim on the part of the State to demand compliance with the public decision of what is for the public good as an unjustifiable tyranny which it is a duty to resist, are in irreconcilable contradiction with others who hold that the safety of the State may rightly override all consideration of private opinion. Eleven hundred conscientious objectors, who refuse to take part in national service of any sort, are said to be undergoing punishment in England; while in New York similar disabilities have been incurred by the followers of Pastor Russell; and Dr Paul Jones, the Bishop of Utah, has been forced to offer to resign his episcopal office[1].

Conscientious objectors seem to have committed themselves to the principle that individual opinion is absolute; they believe they are bound to refuse to act in a way that is inconsistent with this principle. Americans are not inclined to fall into this exaggeration, since, in accepting a written Constitution, they acknowledge national conceptions of right, which are larger and sounder than the vagaries of private opinion. Conscientious ob-

[1] See my article on *Religion in America* in *Nineteenth Century* (1919).

jectors feel justified not only in refusing compliance themselves, but in refusing to engage in
work which would set others free to do what they
cannot conscientiously undertake themselves. They
feel it their duty to carry the practice of passive
resistance to an extreme and to hamper those
activities of the State of which they disapprove.
But the ordinary citizen does not feel that the
individual conscience is absolute; he holds that
persons who live in a country have some duty
towards that country, and that no one has a right
to rely on the soldier of a country for protection,
or to take his share of the food which is provided
by the efforts of the community, unless he is prepared to do something for the community. The
insistence on the individual conscience as absolute
is inconsistent with the teachable spirit which the
Church enjoins, and incompatible with any organisation of the State. It lends itself to mere atomism,
and to the reduction of society to anarchism such
as has come to prevail in Russia.

There was an irreconcilable difference between
the absolutism of the State, as signified in the
worship of the Roman Emperor, and the absolutism
of any community which is so far Christian as to
acknowledge responsibility to God. In pagan times
there was a flat contradiction between the claims
of the State to authority, and the Christian sense
of duty to God, and no reconciliation was possible.
But in modern times there is a possibility of re-

conciliation; and of a constant endeavour to render the State not only nominally, but really Christian, by setting herself to use her influence unselfishly for the welfare of all peoples. A government has enormous powers for putting down mischievous conditions in the country over which it rules; and in the case of Great Britain the government has extraordinary opportunities of promoting the welfare of distant populations, and of influencing other countries. It is impossible for the individual to attempt to exercise such far-reaching influence personally; but in a democratic country he has the opportunity of taking his part in public activities as a citizen. He may determine to repudiate these responsibilities and neglect his opportunities, and to concentrate his thought and life on private duties and private affairs; but his selfish neglect is perilously near the selfish activity of others who are ready to use their public privileges for the promotion of their own interests, and thus to bring about the corruption of the State. Even in heathen times the Christian was far from asserting that he regarded the individual conscience as absolute; a duty of obedience to magistrates in heathen cities is recognised again and again in the Epistles; but in nominally Christian society and in democratic communities the Christian has an opportunity of taking his part in political activities, and of endeavouring to render the society in which he lives more truly Christian. The individual does his

Christian duty not by defying the State, but by
doing his best to discharge the duties of a good
citizen, and thus to influence the society in which
he lives.

53   All questions of ecclesiastical organisation
     have to do with arrangements in place and
time; and they are not in themselves spiritual; and
yet the spiritual cannot work in the world except
through things of sense; "faith cometh by hearing."
The question as to the particular secular organisation which is best fitted to transmit spiritual
truth to future ages is one which cannot be waved
aside or treated as wholly unimportant. It is
also one on which there may be grave differences
of opinion, and there is a diametric opposition
between those who insist that "gathered churches"
offer the only true expression of Christian life, and
those who prefer a form of territorial organisation
such as is exemplified by the parochial system in
England.

It is of course true that the original churches,
as planted by the Apostles in different cities, were
gathered churches; we have very little information
as to their internal organisation or as to the
connection between different churches; but there
need be no dispute about the fact that converts
from among the Jews and the Gentiles were
gathered together by the Apostles, and that in their
meetings they enjoyed the sense of Christian
fellowship and found the opportunity for mutual

edification. It was easy for the Puritans, in Elizabeth's time and under the Stuarts, to contrast the
organisation of parochial affairs and all the secular
activities that were then associated in it, with the
accounts we have of the original condition of the
apostolic churches and their attachment to what
was spiritual. It was possible to regard even
Calvinism with its care for the relief of the poor,
and for the education of the young as a departure
from the apostolic singleness of heart. But there
is a question whether the arrangements, which the
Apostles made for the planting of churches under
their personal supervision, are to be taken as the
models which must be slavishly followed in ecclesiastical organisation under changed conditions of
place and time. Was it imperative as a Christian
duty that parochial organisation should be dis-
placed and that gathered churches which approxi-
mated more nearly to the scriptural model should
be planted in their stead? Did the Apostles institute
a definite system which was to be stereotyped for
all time, or did they plant an organisation which
had the responsibility of maintaining a witness to
Christ through all generations, but with power to
adapt itself so as to discharge its mission more
effectively in changed social conditions?

The Puritans by insisting on reproducing the
form of the apostolic churches in heathen cities were
guilty of a serious oversight in regard to the character of the original churches. They were planted

by the Apostles, and one Apostle at least did not leave them alone to live an independent life, but felt a responsibility for the care of all the churches. The original churches were not associations of spiritually-minded Christians who agreed to form a church; the converts were attracted by teaching which came to them from without, and they did not claim independence of apostolic control. "Came the word "of God out from you? Or came it unto you only?" was the question which S. Paul indignantly asked of the Corinthians; and it is in accordance with apostolic usages to maintain that the business of the Church as Witness for Christ is to form the individual life and the personal opinions, and that no person has a right to claim that he and likeminded individuals shall agree together to make a church.

The life of the body and of its members cannot be completely distinguished; they are intimately connected with one another and react upon each other; unhealthiness in the corporate life is likely to have mischievous effects on one or more of the members, and the excellence of the members is evidence of the fruitfulness of the corporate life. There is, however, an irreconcilable difference in regard to ecclesiastical organisation between those who insist that, because the heart and conscience are the seat of the spiritual, therefore the Christian man is the unit from whom churches are formed by association, and those who recognise that the Church must always be prior to the individual, and that his opinions and habits and practices as a Christian man are formed by the Church.

There is much to be said in favour of either of these principles of organisation. The form of a "gathered church" gives the greatest scope for the consciousness of brotherhood among those who are like-minded, and this is a great strength and support to individual effort; men have constantly fallen back on this principle in forming gilds and associations in addition to territorial organisation; this was the principle to which the Wesleyans desired to remain true, through the eighteenth century, till a parliamentary act[1] forced them to take another line in order to maintain their civil privileges, and they were led to disclaim membership in the Church of England; but the advantages of such a system are exaggerated as soon as we allow ourselves to regard mutual association as the fundamental principle. A body formed on this basis is not well-fitted to discharge the main function of the Church, and to offer a united witness to the world. Where diversity of temperaments and tastes enter into the very foundations of local churches, we are forced to abandon the hope of securing a unity of testimony; there may of course be signs of the work of one Spirit in all denominations, but we can hardly hope that they will of themselves cohere into one body. It is only as

[1] 52 Geo. III, c. 155.

each individual feels the need of trying to adapt himself, not merely of inducing others to adopt his views, that there can ever be a unity of thought and feeling; an identity in the life within, that expresses itself in a united testimony to the world, shows its completeness and fulness by diversity of aspect and by appealing to men of most different temperaments and in various stages of culture.

While there is this difference in regard to the duty of united witness to the world, there is also a difference in the tone of influence which is exercised within, according as we adopt one or the other of these principles of organisation. The man who is conscious of his own conversion, and unites in Christian fellowship with the like-minded, cannot but feel that he has already attained to considerable progress in the knowledge of God; while he may be deeply concerned for others, he is less likely to feel the need of cultivating a teachable spirit than those are who see in the life of the Church an innumerable company of examples of men who served God in different circumstances, and from each of whom there is much to learn. Personal effort to assimilate the truths, in the light of which saintly lives have been lived, is the mark of real catholicity; it refuses to condemn any as wholly evil, who have tried to do God's Will, because of the inadequacy of their knowledge or the strangeness of their sentiments. There has been a revolt from the church of Latin Christendom in many countries; but those Christians are guilty of a strange neglect, who do not try to enter into the thoughts and feelings of such men as S. Thomas Aquinas, S. Thomas à Kempis, or Savonarola, all of whom found satisfaction in the old order. It is by ability to enter into the inner life of professing Christians in the past that we may cultivate readiness to understand and sympathise with the inner life of professing Christians in our own day; and sympathy in the inner life is the essential condition of external agreement.

The principle of treating the individual as the unit from which churches are built up by association, and of regarding this as essential to ecclesiastical organisation, and condemning any other system as in itself wrong, because it seems to be a departure from the original form which Christian life took in heathen cities, has not commended itself by experience; the Puritans did not succeed in their endeavour to supersede the parochial system by gathered churches in Wales and in England. There is need for bringing Christian testimony to bear on every form of organised society, as well as on individual lives; the Church has a mission to the nation as a whole, and she has a mission to each and all of the people in the country; that type of organisation, which keeps this mission in constant view and never allows us to forget it, has much to be said in its favour. It is not a little remarkable that in America, where the conception of gathered churches has been so dominant, there should have arisen such a sense of the need of devising a territorial system and so many movements towards its adoption[1].

54 Intellectual considerations have also been a frequent cause of difference between professing Christians. Religion has an intellectual side; it is necessary to rely on words and thoughts to convey religious truth, and this has necessarily led to the framing of religious formulas, and the construction of theological systems. There has been need of argument in connection with Christian faith and Christian propaganda from the very earliest times; S. Peter exhorts the converts to be "ready always to give an answer to every man that "asketh you a reason of the hope that is in you" (I Peter iii. 15); in every age there has been apologetic literature which has sought to employ reason in the service of faith. We all feel that it is desirable that our thoughts about God should be self-consistent; but when our apprehension is not complete, we can hardly expect to attain to complete consistency of statement. We know in part and we prophesy in part, it is only when that which is perfect is come that we can hope to apprehend the whole in all its parts, and to know even as we are known. Owing to the limitation of human minds we can never be sure that we have terms which are adequate to describe the divine nature; though, as Christian experience grows, we come to be

[1] Cunningham, *Christianity and Politics*, 245.

habituated to terms that are less inadequate than the crudities of primitive thought. Perfect self-consistency can only be secured when we have perfect knowledge; and we may devote ourselves to seeking after consistency of statement, when we would be more worthily employed in endeavouring to attain to fuller experience. Intellectual habits of mind have differed from age to age; the attempts to explain truths about God and His relation to Man, which have been illuminating to the men of one age, have proved unsatisfactory to those who were habituated to a different point of view; Anselm's doctrine of the atonement came home to men who were accustomed to feudal conceptions in all the relations of life; and Aquinas in his doctrine of the sacraments made use of terms which were current in the philosophy of the day, but have greatly fallen into desuetude. It has been a natural result that changes of surroundings and sentiment should give rise to new theological forms of statement; while the intense earnestness of the controversialists has made it very difficult for them to refrain from personal bitterness[1].

The sovereignty of the Supreme Being is a fundamental belief in every form of Theism; but in marking out what is implied in this belief in

[1] Maurice's exposure of the principles which he felt were involved in Mansel's Philosophy must undoubtedly have been irritating, but it does not excuse the expressions which Mansel and his friends used with regard to Maurice personally. Burgon, *Twelve Good Men*, II, 193 n.

Divine Sovereignty, we may find that we conceive of it in different ways, and therefore draw from it very different propositions as to the Divine Character and Divine Working. We may magnify the Divine Being, and treat Omnipotence as if it implied a power to be arbitrary; or on the other hand we may regard the Divine Will as that which is absolutely good, since it is never disturbed by the passions and desires which distract us on earth, and always wills what may be accepted as law universal. When we think of the Supreme Being as the Supreme Good Who is powerful over all, Who has dictated the order of nature, and rules the hearts of kings, we may hope to recognise something of His purpose and to see the ways in which we can best contribute towards realising it in ourselves and in our environment.

The faults in theological controversy have been most conspicuous among those who are inclined to exaggerate the importance of the intellectual element in the religious life, and even to treat religion as merely intellectual, and to identify the spiritual with the intellectual. It is one thing to show that Christian faith is compatible with the exercise of human reason, and another to regard the Father, whom Christ has revealed, as if He were an abstraction of which we know by the exercise of intellectual faculties [1]. It is one thing to treat Christian conduct as compatible with

[1] Coleridge, *Aids to Reflection*, 146.

rational self-love, and another to resolve all motives to Christian action into farseeing regard for self-interest. We have outlived the eighteenth century with its suspicions of enthusiasm, and recognise that devout feeling plays a great part both in the inner lives of individuals and in society. "Chris-"tianity is not a theory or a speculation, but a "life;—not a philosophy of life but a life and a "living process[1]."

Intellectual exaggeration has sometimes taken the form of treating the intellectual element as the basis of all religion; but the practical aspect of religious truth should not be ignored. The intellect cannot grasp in their entirety the manifestations of Himself which God has given, or appreciate His working in the world aright. Locke does not seem to have realised the depth and the bearings of the problems before him[2] when he set himself to come to "an understanding of the Christian Religion" by "undertaking an attentive and unbiassed search "into the Scriptures," of which the result was given to the world in his *Reasonableness of Christianity*. He was ready to identify the spiritual with the intellectual, and to rely on intellectual methods alone in seeking religious truth; and he set an example of a habit of mind which dominated the whole of the eighteenth century in England, and

[1] Coleridge, *Aids to Reflection*, 155.

[2] The doctrine of political institutions in his *Civil Government* is open to similar criticism. Cunningham, *Common Weal*, 32–42.

ramified in many directions. Toland[1] and the
Deists had adopted his principles, and we can
specify some of the channels by which this influence
helped to direct the development of German
theology[2]. Though Stillingfleet set himself to show
the inadequacy of this philosophy, in works which
Bentley re-issued, and Berkeley's doctrine has long
continued to exercise a living influence[3], the
plausibility of Locke's principles rendered them
attractive to orthodox writers who desired to find
an intellectual defence for Christianity. They
treated Natural Religion as commending itself to
the intellect; while they only claimed for Christianity that it was so far analogous to Natural
Religion as to have a high probability. Christianity
was treated as a superstructure which could be
legitimately raised on this intellectual foundation
by the apologetic writers who composed the
Bridgewater Treatises[4]. Advancing knowledge has,
however, shown that Natural Theology cannot be
taken as the basis of a self-consistent body of knowledge; it does not give a key which can solve particular problems; the application of teleology does
not render the workings of Nature intelligible; we

[1] Stillingfleet regarded Toland's *Christianity not mys-
terious* as the legitimate outcome of the principles in Locke's
Essay. Works, III, 521.

[2] A. Tholuck, *Vermischte Schriften*, II, 23 f., 40, 79.

[3] C. E. D'Arcy, Bishop of Ossory, *God and Freedom*, 61.

[4] See my article on *Religion in Cambridge* in the *Nineteenth Century*, June 1918, 1226.

cannot argue in regard to observed phenomena directly from the divine nature and from what we regard as consistent with divine purpose[1]. Since Natural Theology has been discredited as an explanation of the parts of our knowledge, it has ceased to be accepted as the basis of our knowledge of the whole. Our knowledge of God and of His character is not derived from an examination of external nature, but rests on experience of the inner life and on the convictions of those who have tasted and seen that God is good. `

During the eighteenth century there was ample evidence from the Wesleyan movement of the reality of Spiritual Power as working within by personal conviction; and the reality of Spiritual Power working from within outwards into the world was apparent in the great evangelical movements at the end of the century; but the academic theologians of the day disparaged such exhibitions of "enthusiasm[2]" and continued to rely on the

[1] Whewell, *Plurality of Worlds*, 364.

[2] Bp Lavington, who was rightly admired by his contemporaries as a man of "admirable natural parts and sound judgment," was a typical example of this exaggerated reliance on intellect. His *Enthusiasm of Methodists and Papists compared* shows that he viewed religious excitement of any kind as mischievous. He was, as his epitaph in Exeter Cathedral reminds us, "a successful Exposer of Pretence and Enthusiasm" (Polwhele, *Devonshire*, II, 14). S. T. Coleridge, who regarded the Will as essential to spiritual life (*Aids to Reflection*, 99), recognised the importance of feelings and imagination which move the Will (*Ib.* 115).

intellect as exhibiting the truths of Christianity. There was need for the protest of Frederick Maurice against the narrowness of such intellectualism[1]; his living faith—the recognition of Spiritual Power as working in the world to-day—helped him to find the working of Spiritual Power in the past intelligible.

The records of the past are sometimes examined with all the resources of scholarship in the effort to formulate, from the relations of God and Man in the past, true principles as to the relations of God and Man in the present. There is need, however, of an actual appreciation of Spiritual Power, living and vigorous to-day, in order to grasp the full meaning of God's working in the past and to interpret it aright. Biblical studies are in danger of being superficial, if in pursuing them we allow ourselves to dispense with faith[2], and rely on intellect alone[3].

The investigation of the phenomenon of religious life in the past will not suffice to give us guidance for doing Christian duty in the present day. We cannot formulate principles, from the stories of pastoral life in David's time, or even from commercial conditions in the cities of mediaeval Christendom, which can be applied directly to industrial life in the present day. Economic studies may help us as to the choice of means to adopt for pursuing any object, but cannot guide us as to the end at which

[1] Maurice, *Kingdom of Christ*, II, 215; *Life*, I, 83.
[2] Coleridge, *Aids to Reflection*, 285.
[3] *Cambridge University Reporter* (May 7, 1913), XLII, 969.

we ought to aim. Christian faith is needed, as well as science, for social improvement: since faith is spiritual and affords an inspiration to the individual, in any social conditions and under any economic organisation, to try to solve the problems which are presented by his surroundings. There have been countless examples of this endeavour in every age[1], and we can draw courage from these examples even if we find it futile to busy ourselves in searching for principles of Christian Economics[2]. If we should succeed in finding them we should be tempted to try and introduce a modern Theocracy with democratic institutions instead of setting ourselves to live in the fuller light which God will give to those who ask Him.

55   The individual heart and mind is the sphere in which Spiritual Power works; it is only by concentrating attention on the consciousness of individuals personally, that we can detect and do full justice to the working of Spiritual Power. But in this there seems to be a danger, as if the intense conviction of any individual were to be taken as the supreme guide for him. The vagaries of false prophets and of cranks of every sort have professed to rest on immediate inspiration, and we need some corrective.

The individual will be saved from self-deception,

[1] S. R. Maitland, *Dark Ages*, 88, comments on the disregard of S. Eloy's example by modern philanthropists.

[2] On Christian Socialism compare my *Teaching and Influence of F. D. Maurice.*

and from attaching undue importance to his own convictions if he is honestly endeavouring to give expression, by his words and deeds, to the Will of God. It was the characteristic of the prophets of old that they were conscious of a call, not to speak of themselves, but to be the channels of giving a message from God; and the Christian should never allow himself to forget that it is always his duty to endeavour to repress his own self-will, and to lend himself to giving effect to the Will of God. There is an element of humility here which is completely alien to intellectual pride.

But there are also tests to be found in the world around. The Christian will find in external experience of life confirmation of the convictions he cherishes, or else he will find cause to reconsider them. There never can be hope of attaining such demonstration of spiritual truths as is afforded by mathematical analysis of our conception of space, or such empirical proof as is given by observation and experiment within a particular sphere; but there is a possibility of such verification as will give to the man himself confirmation of his belief.

Such confirmation is given to the belief in Spiritual Power, as working in the world in the present and in the past; this is the belief which renders progress intelligible. If we think of the Supreme Being as absolute and arbitrary, the growth of human beings in likeness to Him is unintelligible. If we think of the Universe as a mere machine which works on regularly in all its parts, the progress of Man is unintelligible. It only becomes intelligible when we believe that the progress of Man has its ultimate reason in the purpose of God; and that each man, by making the most of his opportunities can do something to carry out the purpose of God. The progress of the race confirms the Christian belief in the purpose of God, and in the Christian sense of the responsibility of Man.

III. COLLECTIVE EFFORT

56   The conviction as to the reality of Spiritual Power, which is felt personally, has been confirmed because this belief renders the progress of the human race in the past intelligible. It is also confirmed because it gives insight and guidance for the doing of duties in the present; its truth is exemplified in so far as it works. By conscious endeavours after collective effort, we may be able to give the most effective united witness to Christ.

It is important that we should, so far as possible, lay aside the differences which divide Christians; but it is impossible that religious life should be organised in the world so as to be entirely without political, or historical or intellectual affinities. It is impossible that these should be dispensed with altogether; political, ecclesiastical and intellectual causes are likely enough to produce recurring difficulties in the future, as they have done in the past. They have their greatest strength in organised

denominations; and it is extremely difficult for any
such body to admit that its very existence has been
due to insistence on some point, which is now seen
to be of quite subordinate importance, and to
disown its own past and agree to corporate re-
union. But it is possible for each individual to
throw himself heartily into work for objects of
which others realise the importance, without lay-
ing stress on points of difference which are not
relevant to the matter in hand. It is by concentration on practical efforts that the difficulties
which arise from political or historical or intellectual
causes may be, not solved, but evaded, and that a
great measure of co-operation may be secured. As
has been finely said, "All difficulties solvuntur
"ambulando for those who walk with God."

57   There are two distinct instruments which
lie ready to hand, with the view of securing
farther advance and of taking steps in progress; the
forces of compulsion and of attraction are quite
different, but they each have a place; the difficulty
is to find how each may be used in turn so as to
effect the best result on the whole. Compulsion
applies to external conditions, and the State is
entrusted with the power to use it. There may be
the greatest differences of opinion as to the ends
for which it may be prudently brought to bear;
and as to the means which are most expedient for
promoting these ends. Ought the State to endeavour to promote thrift among the population? Is

it wise to do so by encouraging Friendly Societies or should it compel everyone to insure? These are difficulties which have been much discussed in recent years; and they have revealed the fact that there is much more agreement as to the evils which the State should endeavour to put down, than as to the directions in which it may wisely attempt to force men to lead godly or sober lives. In bringing compulsion to bear, considerations of expediency can never be left wholly out of sight; it is not enough, when insisting on any measure, to be well intentioned; it is necessary to consider the probabilities of success and the mischief that may be incidental to the attempt, or the reaction that may result from a failure. Through the Middle Ages and under the Puritan theocracies, there was no scruple about the use of force to secure the extension of Christendom, or to enforce a high tone in society; but experience has not encouraged efforts to secure spiritual aims by coercive measures; those who rely on force must be content to produce external conformity, and not to aim at anything deeper.

There is likelihood of a very general agreement as to the importance of putting down positive evils when we can reach them. The progress of science has given us the means of coping with mischief of many sorts, which our forefathers could not attempt to deal with; and we are inclined to be enthusiasts for making war against disease, and for sanitary reform. Law and Police are the agents by which the State endeavours to put down crime within; and the Army and Navy attempt to afford security from foreign attack. From the Elizabethan age onwards, there has been serious effort to put down the evils of poverty, by paying attention to the national food-supply and the opportunities of employment. The development of insurance has given the means of guarding against the troubles which arise from the uncertainty in human affairs. Compulsion is exercised by the State to ensure that if these evils cannot be put down altogether, they shall at least be guarded against.

While there is general agreement among all citizens, who have any desire for the public good, that it is desirable to put down and guard against such evils, there may be much question as to the expediency of our efforts. Many people, who look at the moral effect on character and on the results in the long run, fear that rescuing the labourer from the risk of privation may diffuse dependence on the State, and weaken personal effort; or they are alarmed lest the maintenance of armies may be provocative and tend to bring about breaches of the peace between nations. It is clear enough that the results of employing coercion must differ in different societies with different habits and customs; and for this very reason there is great difficulty in seeing at any moment how it is wisest to act; but there is a very wide field in which coercion is available as a useful means of putting down the evils that beset human life. Men, who have little in common religiously or intellectually, may work together for such aims; and the Christian man may find ready co-operation for doing the duties of citizenship among those whose personal religious life, if it exists at all, is very different from his own. The Christian consciousness of responsibility ought to be an effective support to men who are endeavouring to enforce attention to what is expedient for the putting down of evils, and who are themselves ready to co-operate with all others, apart from personal considerations, in doing the duties of citizenship personally.

58   But though compulsion by the State and coercion may do much to secure and maintain any step of progress that has been won, they are of little use in making a step forward or initiating progress. It is not always possible to enforce well-intended legislation. Compulsion is an effective instrument for maintaining what is generally admitted to be good for society, but its success depends on careful administration and its results are often superficial.

The initiative in progress has generally come from some individual who has cherished a new ideal, and has been at pains to experiment on the possibility of bringing it into effect. It is necessary, if improvements in society are not merely to be superficial but are to be heartily accepted and if there is to be actual progress, that attention should be given to the inner life of the citizens, and that they should be attracted to what is good, and not merely coerced into discarding what is mischievous and bad. Where the tone of society is high, there will be comparatively little need for the enforcement of penalties; the more the attraction of good is felt, the more is it possible to dispense with inspection and compulsion, and to leave the citizens to themselves in the confidence that they will conform to the public good. It is necessary to set before men higher ideals, and to inspire them to endeavour to make them their own and act up to them.

There are many agencies which lay stress on the power of attraction and try to make use of it, and hold up comforts and satisfactions that are worth striving for,—Benefit Societies, Building Societies and Friendly Societies of all sorts; of each it is true that they do their best work, when they change the character of their members personally, and render them less eager about particular material benefits, and more deeply imbued with the Friendly Society spirit, and the consciousness of the power they possess to help one another. Every community finds advantage in the loyalty of its members, and from being able to count on their character; public spirit is the only corrective which can preserve any form of polity from corruption; spirit and discipline are the qualities which render an army efficient, and they are not only valuable in war, but necessary for effective service of the State in time of peace. The moulding of the inner life is the work which the Church is specially commissioned to do; she can do this efficiently, since she holds up the highest ideal of manhood and seeks to persuade each man to adopt it as his own, and to endeavour to realise it personally. It is the function of the Church to witness to Christ as the ideal for every life, and to help men to feel the attractive force of His example.

There is a danger in every age that the Church should not be true to this spiritual mission, but should be secularised; and we have no immunity from that danger now. We are so impatient of the slowness of growth, and of efforts to mould the human will and to attract to higher ideals; we are anxious to force the pace and compel men for their own good. But there is a danger of mistaking our aim if we allow ourselves to be in a hurry. Probably no man in the nineteenth century took a larger part in the initiating of movements for social reform than Frederick Maurice—both in guiding the co-operative movement, and in starting such organisations for promoting education as the Working Men's College, and Queen's College in Harley Street. But those who look back on him and his achievements with admiration, do not always appear to be aware of his intense horror of any tendency in the Church to discard the Spiritual Commission, which can effect a transformation in human beings that shall be permanent, and to direct her energies instead to temporary alleviations and superficial pallia-

tions. The Church in her corporate capacity does
not do well to relegate to a second place her efforts
to foster a better life within, and devote herself to
the work of readjusting the social mechanism; other
agencies are quite as well fitted for forming public
opinion. The Friends regard those who persistently
defy the public conscience as heroes; but the
methods, by which they endeavour to awaken the
public conscience to a sense of wrong doing in
regard to them, are closely akin to those of political
agitation. Most pitiable is it, if the clergy allow
themselves "to take up social questions," not
because they really desire to do their best to effect
a permanent cure, but because they hope that they
can advertise the Church as the friend of the
working classes, and induce them to give more
heed to her teaching. It is the mission of the
Church to bring Spiritual Power to work on individuals personally, so that having first given
themselves to the Lord they may be more eager
to do His will, as they themselves see it, in all
the relations of citizenship.

59 All the members of Christ's Church are
called to set forth by their lives the faith
that is in them as a present power, that men seeing
their good works, as citizens or in their special
vocation, whatever it is, may glorify their Father
which is in Heaven. All are called on to be ready
to confess Christ before men, and to use the
opportunities that occur for thus testifying to Him

according to their ability. The recognition of this duty on the part of all the members of Christ's Church, has raised the question as to the special functions of the clergy, and whether there is any meaning in setting them apart to minister. Laymen devote themselves to Biblical Science; it is not a field of scholarship in which the clergy have any monopoly; and the testimony of laymen, as to their personal spiritual experience and their sense of what religion is to them, is often far more impressive than clerical preaching; it conveys a sense of reality that is contagious.

But the special work of the clergy lies in the fact that they not only have a duty in the present, but that they are trustees of the spiritual heritage from the past, which it is their duty to hand on in undiminished power to the future. It is their duty to keep the memory of Christ and His earthly life green, that the men of each age and every place may have the opportunity of living in the light He has given. We are all apt to be carried away by the fashions of our own time, be they artistic, or intellectual or political; and we can see as we look back, how these various fashions have given special applications to the Christianity of each age, which were not necessarily fitted to impress other ages; monasticism seems to have had its day and makes no widespread appeal now, though community life still exercises a strong attraction[1]. Though the

[1] R. A. Cram, *Ruined Abbeys of Great Britain*, 273.

spirit of chivalry has doubtless been awakened in hundreds who have sacrificed themselves for their country to-day, the Military Orders were for an age and are not likely to be revived. But there is a Christian heritage for all time; it is in the preservation of that heritage and of the meaning which other ages have found in the life of Christ, that the special function of the clergy consists. They have undertaken this trust, and the more they are conscious of their trusteeship, and of their duty as good stewards to bring forth things both new and old, the better will they discharge their function in the Church. There has been a wonderful revolution during the last century in the disregard of terrorism as a religious force, and increasing reliance on the declaration of the attractive power of the Love of God[1]. Each age has experiences of its own, and is apt to resent the influence of the past, to rebel against the "dead hand," or against the phraseology which was appropriate to other habits of thought. It is the task of the clergy to distinguish, and to abandon the pedantries and anachronisms which give unnecessary offence, while maintaining the tradition which God's Spirit has used as a living power in every age; they are not merely called on to express their personal experience or their personal opinions, but to declare the faith of Christ's Church. At their ordination the clergy are set apart to undertake the responsibility of this trusteeship

[1] Cunningham, *Increase of True Religion*, 35.

and solemnly commissioned to be faithful dispensers of God's Holy Word and Sacraments.

There have been men at many times and in diverse places who have claimed to have outlived Christianity, and to have entered on a plane on which they can, like Eucken, dispense with the historical setting of spiritual truth. They are so conscious of divine power in delivering them from sin, that they can be indifferent to any external manifestations of divine power, such as our Lord's Resurrection. They are so conscious of divine power constantly working within, that they are indifferent to the unique manifestation of spiritual power in the Incarnation. However we may fear the dangers of self-deception ourselves we need not deny the possibility of such attainment in others. There are hints in the New Testament of the possibilities of Spiritual Power beyond our knowledge, and apart from earthly things altogether. It is not for us to know the times and the seasons which the Father has put in His own power. S. Paul found himself caught into the third heaven and heard unspeakable words which it was not lawful to utter. A day will dawn when our Lord shall deliver up the Kingdom unto His Father, that God may be all in all. But our duty here and now is that of rendering earthly things subservient to spiritual purposes and powers[1]. It may suffice for those who are conscious of special gifts to have faith to themselves and to

[1] Coleridge, *Aids to Reflection*, 123.

God (1 Cor. xiv. 28); but it is by maintaining the faith in Spiritual Power as manifested in the person of Jesus Christ that the war against evil is to be waged, that men are to be attracted to place themselves under His banner, to discipline themselves to take their place in His ranks, and thus to have a part in the work of Christ's Church militant here on earth.

60   The progress of the human race in command over nature has been extraordinary; we see it in the difference between the uncertainties of savage tribes who rely on the food which nature provides, and the organised resources of modern society. But behind it all and through it all we can trace the signs of spiritual progress, which renders material progress intelligible and seems to give the impulse which initiates it and carries it on. We can trace its beginnings in the reliance of Abraham in special crises on Some One whom he could trust for all time; we see how this confidence in Unseen Power has come to be felt as a constant possession; we read how some men have lost the sense of antagonism, in the consciousness that they are themselves the instruments of that Power, and may themselves enter into companionship with God. Those who attain to a consciousness of their Sonship will not only enjoy a peace which passes all understanding, but will find courage to acquit themselves manfully in all the complexities of life.

INDEX

For EU product safety concerns, contact us at Calle de José Abascal, 56–1°,
28003 Madrid, Spain or eugpsr@cambridge.org.

www.ingramcontent.com/pod-product-compliance
Ingram Content Group UK Ltd.
Pitfield, Milton Keynes, MK11 3LW, UK
UKHW012331130625
459647UK00009B/219